The Presentation

Being able to communicate your message to people has never been more important. This book is for people who aren't just wanting to make money - they want to make a difference.

CATHY BURKE
CEO The Hunger Project Australia

Brilliant book Joey! I love how you bring together the art and the science of speaking to show people how to build a powerful (and profitable) speaking business that's chock full of passion.

DARYL GRANT, Author of *Our Internet Secrets* and *7-Figure Speaker*, Featured on Channel 9, A Current Affair.

Never before has there been such a complete overview of the business of speaking. If you have a message to share this book will help you monetise it simply and effectively. Jo has written this as an industry insider, it would take years to discover what Jo has outlined so perfectly in this book.

DANIEL PRIESTLEY, Author of *How to Become a Key Person of Influence* and Entrepreneur, London, UK

Joanna Martin is a master of the speaking business - if you're serious about speaking and have a message to share, then this book will help you realise your full potential. It really is the complete overview of the business of speaking. Read it now and profit!

MICHAEL SHEARGOLD Author, Speaker, Coach, Blogger and Entrepreneur

Before I met Joanna Martin - I was a brilliant speaker :-)

Then Jo showed me how to - not only maintain the positive feedback I'd been getting - but to turn that applause into ongoing streams of cash.

Jo - where were you 20 years ago?

Thank goodness for anyone in the speaking arena you're there to guide them to the success they deserve

Thanks - a million (Oh - actually much more than a million!)

PETER THOMSON
"The UK's Most Prolific Information Product Creator"

Simply brilliant! Joanna's 7-Shift Effective Presentation Formula alone makes the entire book worth its weight in gold.

JANET BECKERS, Wonderful Web Women, Australia

It's about time this book was written. It's a much awaited overview on the lifestyle and business of speaking, and Joanna demonstrates just how simple it can be...

BEN ANGEL, The Agent of Influence, Author of *Sleeping Your Way to the Top in Business*, Australia

THE PRESENTATION PROFITS BLUEPRINT

by Dr Joanna Martin

FAST
WORLD
PUBLISHING GROUP

Disclaimer

All the information, techniques, skills and concepts contained within this publication are of the nature of general comment only, and are not in any way recommended as individual advice. The intent is to offer a variety of information to provide a wider range of choices now and in the future, recognising that we all have widely diverse circumstances and viewpoints. Should any reader choose to make use of the information contained herein, this is their decision, and the contributors (and their companies), authors and publishers do not assume any responsibilities whatsoever under any conditions or circumstances. It is recommended that the reader obtain their own independent advice.

Any income statements and examples are not intended to represent or guarantee that everyone will achieve the same results. Each individual's success will be determined by his or her desire, dedication, effort, and motivation. There are no guarantees you will duplicate the results stated here, recognising that any business endeavour has inherent risk for loss of capital.

FIRST EDITION 2012

Copyright © 2012 Shift Enterprises Pty Ltd

All rights reserved. No part of this publication may be reproduced, stored in a retrieval system, or transmitted in any form or by any means, electronic, mechanical, photocopying, recording or otherwise, without prior written permission from the publisher.

National Library of Australia
Cataloguing-in-Publication entry:

Martin, Dr Joanna.
The Presentation Profits Blueprint / Dr Joanna Martin

ISBN   9780987199928 (pbk.)

1.Marketing 2. New business enterprises, 3. Small business — Management.

658.8708

Published by Fast World Publishing Group
PO Box 6864 GCMC 9726, QLD Australia
Email: info@fastworldpublishing.com.au
Website: www.FastWorldPublishing.com.au

DEDICATION

To the difference makers: those who know their life is for a purpose, and those with the courage to leave their mark.

CONTENTS

Acknowledgements ix
Bonuses xi
Introduction xiii

PART 1: Turn Your Words Into Wealth 1

  1. Presentation Profits Blueprint 3
  2. Great v. Profitable 7
  3. Speaking is a Business 9
  4. Confidence 21
  5. Monetizing your gifts 25
  6. Beyond Your Comfort Zone 29
  7. Money Mindset 35

PART 2: The Seven Profit Principles You Must Master To Make Massive, Leveraged Income From Your Passion Through Speaking 41

  8. The Seven Profit Principles 43
  9. Profit Principle One: Passion 45
 10. Profit Principle Two: People 63
 11. Profit Principle Three: Promise 79
 12. Profit Principle Four: Propagate 93
 13. Profit Principle Five: Products 113
 14. Profit Principle Six: Presentation 133

15. Profit Principle Seven: Profit 175
16. Putting the Blueprint Into Action...................... 187

About the author 191

ACKNOWLEDGEMENTS

It really has been a long time coming, this book. But now that it's done I feel everything is at last in its place!

For a big picture gal like me, the attention to detail required to take my book to publication is quite beyond me. I couldn't have done it without the tireless support and dedicated energy of the entire Shift team. To Jo Harrison, Donna Powell, Daniel Coffey, Hannah Davis, Stuart Brann, Andrea Pennisi, Kim Browning, Tamara Norwood, and Vanessa Rothwell – I am truly blessed to have your support and I thank you for the space you allow me.

To Stephanie DeMizio – thank you for your incredible input in pulling all the threads together! I can't even imagine how this would have occurred without you.

To Glenn Walford and the team at Fast World Publishing Group – thank you for taking me under your wing, and for the huge effort you've put into creating a book that looks this good!

To my mother, Claire Stride – a huge thank you for encouraging me no matter what crazy idea I brought home. To my stepfather, Roger Stride – thank you for supporting me even when you didn't understand what I was up to. And to my father, Peter Martin – thank you for showing me that true sales is about a commitment to making people's lives better, even if it hurts.

To my sisters Kath and Em, who are always ready to pick holes in my projects for the sake of a cheap laugh – thank you for causing me to keep it real!

And to my husband, Greg Elliott – Thank you for your ceaseless support and encouragement, and for the gentle way you keep me stretching and growing. I don't know what I ever did to deserve someone as patient as you – I will be forever in your debt!

Finally to you, my reader – I thank you in advance for the difference you make in the world. My hope is that this book makes some small difference for you, so that you can make an even bigger difference in your community.

BONUSES

Bonus Resources – valued at more than $342

I can't give you everything you need to know about speaking in one small book (though I really have tried!), so I've created a special website for you with loads of extra goodies to help you grow your income through speaking. You'll find:

- ✓ Training videos on how to apply the lessons from this book
- ✓ Template order forms you can model for your own presentations
- ✓ My audience analysis checklist, with 14 questions to ask yourself before you design any presentation
- ✓ Loads of other useful resources to help you grow your business.

To check out the resources page go to:
www.PresentationProfitsBlueprint/bonusresources.

Bonus Gift: Intensive Online Training Session – valued at $67

As a special thank you for investing in this book, I'd like to invite you to join me on a webinar very soon for a 90 minute, intensive online training session to help you to put the Presentation Profits Blueprint into action.

This "Next Steps" webinar is held regularly throughout the year to hold your hand and guide you step by step through actually implementing the strategies and techniques you will learn in this book. On the webinar we'll cover:

- The main reason most speakers fail
- How to apply the 7 Profit Principles in your industry, regardless of where you're starting from
- How to decide your personalized step-by-step path through the Principles, and where you should focus first
- The fastest way to make new income within the next 30 days.

So whether you want to read the book first, or join us straight away for this training, you'll find the details of the next webinar training at www.PresentationProfitsBlueprint. com/nextstep.

INTRODUCTION:
THE SPEAKING SHIFT

Picture yourself in front of a captivated audience. All eyes are on you – everyone is waiting with bated breath for what you're going to say next. With every word you speak you can sense the approval and adoration of the crowd; you feel yourself connected to them on a higher level that transcends time and space...

Okay, maybe it's not *that* dramatic.

There is power in speaking. Speaking allows us to share our message with so much passion that we can move people to take action and improve their lives. And if it's done with authenticity, honesty and common sense, the good news is there are also profits.

I've written this book to show you how your commitment to inspire and empower others can bring you a life-changing income. This is not just another book on *how* to speak, but a step-by-step blueprint for creating the lifestyle of your dreams *through* speaking. Imagine waking up every day knowing that you are living your best possible life. Would that give you an enormous sense of freedom?

Speaking is the most profitable business skill you can ever learn, and I credit it as the reason for the lifestyle I'm living today. Let me take a step back and explain how I got to be in this position where I have the privilege of sharing my knowledge with you. It's been an interesting road to say the least!

One of the first things you should know about me is that I've never been a 'get through life' kind of gal. I am a go-getter and hold myself to a very high standard. I am now a professional speaker, but I actually started my working life as a medical doctor in Tasmania, Australia, before discovering that I really didn't love what I was doing. Being a doctor didn't light me up; I was only going through the motions.

After losing one of my favorite patients, a beautiful, young, Irish, pixie-like mother of two, I realized that time was too precious to spend going through the motions. I stopped and took a long, hard look at what I was doing with my life.

Have you ever been so shaken up emotionally by an experience that you go looking for answers? You try to make sense of what is happening and find a deeper meaning. That's certainly what I was doing when I made the decision to leave medicine and follow my heart.

Ever since the sixth grade, I've had a passion for performing, so the year after choosing not to be a doctor anymore, I ran away to drama school in Sydney. I attended the prestigious Actors Centre Australia – alumni include Nicole Kidman and Hugh Jackman – and it was magical; I was having an amazing time. However, about six months into my school term, I looked at myself and thought, 'What difference am I making here?'

It was while dealing with my inner conflict of loving acting but feeling I needed to make more of a difference in the world that I went to my very first personal development seminar. Until this point I didn't even know there was a seminar industry. But here were thousands of people who called themselves speakers, sharing their passion, making a difference and performing. I was in heaven and I was hooked!

That first seminar was the catalyst for a series of actions that soon followed. I quickly immersed myself in personal development, became a coach and served as a trainer for a well-known personal development specialist. My life became a whirlwind. I was traveling all over the world, making a huge impact, but I was missing someone very special to me. To continue on the path I was on meant that I had to be away from my partner, Greg, for months at a time. I realized that while I loved what I was doing, I also loved him. It was time to make another decision that would significantly change the direction of my life yet again.

So you see, I am not a 'get through life' kind of person. And you don't have to be that way either. You don't have to settle for anything other than what makes your heart soar. I want more for you. I want you to be extraordinary.

I have written this book to guide you through the system I have developed, so you can leverage your speaking, create passive income streams and build a lifestyle from your speaking business.

BLUEPRINT IN ACTION SNAPSHOT

Hi Jo! Here's a triple thanks coming your way.

Thanks for working with us on our Elegant Business Model on the cruise. It really made sense and it's a sensational model for us.

Secondly, thanks for helping us to get bums on seats for our event. We used your principle of 'There's not one way to get 100 people in a room but 100 ways to get one person in a room' and it worked. We were sold out one week before the event. So thanks number two!

And finally, in the lead up to the event I hadn't spoken or sold for over eight months. So guess what we did – we went back to the Presentation Profits Blueprint. It was the absolute best blueprint that Pam and I used to go through step-by-step to build the presentation and to build the close.

We were and still are excited and wrapped. Not only did we help so many people, but we also closed over $60,000 of new business, and for us that is a fantastic stepping-stone. Leading on from that, using the new Elegant Business Model, we are set to make over $100,000 in 30 days! Thanks so much!

Steve Brossman
Video and Relationship Marketing Strategist
Sydney, Australia
www.magneticdigitalmarketing.com

PART
ONE

TURN YOUR WORDS INTO WEALTH

1

PRESENTATION PROFITS BLUEPRINT

Buckle your seatbelts because you are about to learn the blueprint to make massive profits as a speaker and attain the lifestyle of your dreams. I'll be straight with you – there are many ways to get this wrong. You'll want to participate in this program by taking notes, completing the exercises and measuring your progress. Doing the right things at the right time is also important, so make sure you read this book in its entirety, from beginning to end.

This blueprint is designed to support you through all of the phases of building your speaking business to ensure you know where you should be spending your time *right now*. This will be different for everyone depending on where you are in the process.

Some of you reading this book are complete newbies to the world of speaking. You may be excited and a little nervous about entering the industry. You may still be working for someone else and are just warming up to the idea of owning your own business. Be proud. Be strong. You have a distinct advantage. Do you want to know why? You don't have to *un*learn anything! If you have an open mind and are committed to excellence, you will gain not only a sense of possibility for what you can accomplish, but an understanding of the step-by-step system on how to do it.

For those of you who are intermediate, meaning you have already read other books, taken courses or completed training on the subject of speaking, you will learn how to increase your profits by leveraging your time more efficiently. I'm talking to my small business owners, service providers, consultants and coaches. Some of you may be dabbling with the idea of speaking, while still working nine-to-five. If you follow the blueprint, you will learn how to accelerate your transition into a full time speaker in your current area of expertise.

My seasoned vets, those of you who are already making money from speaking but want to turn it into a real profit center, you will learn how to maximize your income, better manage your resources and reclaim your lifestyle. You will gain the ultimate competitive advantage.

BLUEPRINT IN ACTION SNAPSHOT

One of the techniques I learned from Joanna Martin made me over £5,000 in 23 minutes. Some of the things you're going to learn here, many speakers don't know about. Some of the secrets you're going to learn, a lot of speakers just don't do. If you want to make money from speaking or be selling your idea to an audience, listen to what Joanna says!

John Lee
Property Investor and Speaker
www.wealthdragons.co.uk

Whatever your level, whether you are new or already speaking, there are going to be distinctions that you can take away from this book and apply right away for immediate results. But you have to be in action. You must create momentum. When you successfully complete a task that you've never done before or you generate a new stream of income, the sense of, "Wow! I've gotten somewhere!" is going to be so overwhelming that it will cause you to want that sensation again and again. You want to strive to make that feeling a habit that will then ripple out and make every action you take after that much easier.

There may be times during this journey that you'll hit a roadblock. I can promise that if you do, it will most likely be due to your mindset. I'm sure you've had opportunities and experiences where you've been learning something and you've recognized it as familiar, and that little voice inside your head has said, "Yes, I have heard that before. I know that." Those two words, *I know*, will shut down your mind faster than anything else.

What I would like you to do instead of thinking "I know" when you read something you might have read or heard before is to ask in its place, "Have I created a result with that distinction yet?" Please underline, highlight or star this question. **Have I created a result with that distinction yet?** If you haven't fully implemented the distinction, really put yourself out on the line to make it happen. You do not know it until you integrate it. Period.

GREAT V. PROFITABLE

I will let you in on a secret. There are a number of famous speakers out there who appear to be making loads of money. In fact, they are making huge revenues, but their margins are so low that the profit they take home hardly makes it worth the effort.

I have been doing talks and presentations since 2003, but in 2005 I became a full time, focused, professional speaker. During the following year I discovered just how much money could be made in speaking – the *right kind* of speaking.

In that year alone, I made over $1.25 million in sales from stage. I realized the real money was not in being paid a fee to deliver a speech, but in having products and services to sell from stage at each presentation or training you deliver.

For the first three years of my professional speaking career, I was on the road for 513 days, and on stage speaking and selling for 373 of them. By the middle of 2007, I had spent over 3,544 hours on stage. I was also consulting with businesses, resulting in total revenue of over $47 million. I managed all of this before my 30th birthday. Those three years changed my life.

While I generated a large sum of income during that time, I also nearly burnt out. And after that long run, I decided to do something radical. I took nine months off to sample retirement, during which time I was approached by dozens of my old students asking me to teach them what I knew about making money through speaking. I initially refused because I was hesitant to enter an industry already overflowing with speakers teaching presentation skills. I argued that the world didn't need another person teaching how to be a really great presenter. However, something kept nagging at me. You see, there were so many great presenters out there who had no money in their bank accounts. So after careful consideration, I determined the key that set me apart from everyone else was that I wasn't just teaching the tools to become a great speaker; I was teaching the tools to become a *profitable* speaker. Big difference.

Denise Duffield-Thomas
So - I ran a small workshop today, used your system and converted 80% of the room. My offer was obviously irresistible! Thank you for the inspiration!

02 April at 16:12 · Unlike · Comment

www.deniseduffieldthomas.com
Coach and author of Lucky Bitch

SPEAKING IS A BUSINESS

I am infinitely grateful to my Million Dollar Master Class, my preferred and high-end clients, for the lessons I have learned from them – the roadblocks, slip-ups and successes that have allowed me to put together this roadmap for you. It is through supporting them during this process that I've been able to distill the foolproof formula for presentation profits. I only hope they don't mind since, after all, they paid between $19,000 and $100,000 per person for this information! Please forgive me guys...

What I really want to emphasize to you, as I did with my Master Class, is that speaking is a business. It's so versatile that you can integrate speaking into every industry. Listed below are the five core components that are needed for any business to be successful, and all of them can be served through speaking.

1. Research and Development
2. Marketing
3. Sales (products, services, programs)
4. Product Creation/Manufacturing
5. Product Delivery.

Let's take a closer look at them now.

Research and Development

In your professional life, you need to be constantly innovating and moving forward, finding out what the market needs and wants. Before you create a new product or service, ask yourself:

- What are the latest themes in the marketplace?
- What is shifting?
- What are the current economic conditions and what is being forecast for the future?

Speaking is probably the quickest and easiest way to get started in business. Once you choose a topic and begin speaking publicly, you instantly have a platform to ask your questions directly to your market and receive immediate feedback. I'm talking about addressing small clubs and networking groups without the intention of selling anything. You can share your message and ask your audience, "Would you like to learn more? What interests you the most about my subject matter? What type of product would you like me to create?"

We'll talk more about this when we get to Principle Five in Part Two, but, as a general rule of thumb, do not create a product until you've sold it. You only know that someone is going to buy your product when you've sold the first one!

BLUEPRINT IN ACTION SNAPSHOT

I have been a lifetime employee and have been procrastinating on starting my own business for at least 5 to 10 years, printed business cards, been to numerous seminars and listened to many great mentors. Now after just three weeks listening to Joanna and being part of her Silver Mentoring program, I am in business. I sent one email out last night and have my first teleseminar in three weeks, have registrations already and am actively chasing speaking gigs– it's scary but absolutely exhilarating at the same time! Thanks Joanna for the great information and motivation!

Kym Heffernan
Speaker and Business Consultant
MROI Marketing
www.kymheffernan.com
www.marketingmakeover.com.au

Marketing

In any business there are two components to your marketing:

1. You need to have a strong brand.
2. You need a system for attracting new prospects.

From a branding perspective, nothing positions you more perfectly for growing your business than stepping onto a stage and speaking, because you get on the spot credibility and expert status. Imagine there is a line at the front of your stage. I call this imaginary line the 'credibility line'. On one side of the line there is the audience. On the other side of the line (on the stage) there is the expert. That is you. You are the authority when you are on the stage, simply because *you are the one on stage!*

BLUEPRINT IN ACTION SNAPSHOT

Just thought we would drop you a quick note to let you know how my second ever speaking engagement went. I was invited to be one of the guest speakers at design EX, Australia's biggest design expo, which was held at the Sydney Convention Centre. Not one to do things by half, I decided to give myself a massive challenge – to accept the invitation to speak and launch my design book at design EX, plus get two of the designers who are featured in the book involved in the presentation too!

Deep down, I was hoping no one would turn up as I was and still am nervous as hell, but as it turned out my presentation was sold out! That's right – SOLD OUT! And people had to pay $65 to hear me speak too, which I didn't find out until the last minute!

I did a book signing afterwards at the bookshop, and lots of people who attended the presentation came down to get their own autographed copy. This has already led to leads to future speaking engagements.

The directors of some tertiary institutions are eager for me to share with their students my experience and what I learnt from researching the top designers for the book, to inspire them to realize their own dreams can come true too. Inspire is my word that I used when Heidi and I attended your Presentation Secrets presentation in Brisbane back in late Feb, so to be able to start doing this soon is incredible. I can't wait!

I wasn't allowed to 'sell' as such, but just talking to the audience about success, and how you can achieve anything you want in life, led to people buying the books in droves. We almost sold out of books throughout the three-day expo, too, which was fantastic! We're organizing a 'bigger than Ben Hur' online launch too, so we'll keep you posted.

We wanted to share the good news with you guys and thank you all for being such a wonderful source of inspiration to both Heidi and me.

David Cuschieri
Interior Designer, Sydney, Australia
www.cuschieridesigns.com.au

For example, if you're an accountant by trade and you want to stand out from your competition, get on a stage and teach business owners how to handle their finances. Keep it simple. Address people who need and want to learn your content. If they have to choose between a guy they looked up in the yellow pages, and you – the expert they heard speak at the networking event last month – who are they going to choose? You, of course!

The lifeblood of all business is sales, and every person in every audience is a potential client. Even if you never close a sale from stage, you always want to walk away from the scene of a presentation with everyone's contact information. They give you the gift of their time, to listen to what you have to say, so if you offer them a free newsletter or other gift as a way of keeping in touch, you will find that between 60 – 100% of your audience will give you their business card.

BLUEPRINT IN ACTION SNAPSHOT

I've been in your Silver Mentoring Program since last summer, and started with the Blueprint series. I began adapting the principles in autumn by starting a series of webinars about my topic, "negotiation",and then I released an open seminar, which will take place in February. And all works well.

I have more subscribers on my lists than ever; the seminar is almost full. In today's webinar I'm going to sell the last seats, based on your sales process.So, thank you again.

Wolfgang Boenisch
Speaker and Negotiation Trainer
Hamburg, Germany
www.wolfgangboenisch.com

Sales

Whatever industry you're in, you must sell. Whether it's your ideas, services, programs or products, you are always selling. As a speaker, one of the greatest skills you could ever learn is closing sales from the stage. Now, you may not see how this applies to your current profession, so let me give you an example.

When I was a coach, I used the traditional sales process of networking to find prospects. I connected with people individually and if they seemed interested in what I did, I invited them to a free first taster session. This method worked many times, but what happened most frequently was I'd call them to schedule and they'd never call back. They were so excited when I first approached them, but I never heard from them again. When people get something for free, they become skeptical and think there is a catch. They think it's too good to be true.

Seminars are perceived to be high-pressure environments, but in actuality they are less intimidating than one-to-one sessions. The beauty of them, as a speaker, is that you can educate your audience and give them enough information to make a decision on their own terms. When I ran my very first event, I invited all 60 people in my Microsoft Outlook address book (you have to start somewhere!). Surprisingly, the people who showed up were not my clients – the people who I expected to be there because they knew me already – but the people who had expressed so much excitement but had never scheduled their free appointment. Their mindset was that it was less pressure to attend a group function where they could decide for themselves if I was the real deal. I had eight whole people in the room that day! I closed one sale and I made $795. I was on cloud nine!

"But," you might think, "this doesn't work in my industry." Well, let me give you another example. I have a client who sells security lighting – lights that are used outside of commercial and residential properties. He began speaking to groups of property developers to teach them about external lighting, to help educate them on his product. He would invite them to a presentation and he kept it very informal. At the end, he wouldn't sell them anything, but instead he would offer the opportunity to book an appointment for a follow up meeting. Because he had already established a relationship and educated these developers, he could now usually close the sale in the next appointment, rather than in three or four. He leveraged his sales activities by making that initial introduction to a group, rather than one-to-one.

Speaking and sales make a great team. We will talk more about this throughout the book.

BLUEPRINT IN ACTION SNAPSHOT

I'm a naturopath in a small country town of only 9000, and when I started I was only making money through one-to-one consulting. Through the Shift System I have been able to deliver my message to groups, in the same time as it takes me to do it with an individual – which means that where I used to make $200 per hour, in my first presentation I made $10,000 in 90 minutes!

The best part is I now work 2 1/2 days a week, and take 80% of all school holidays off to spend with my children. I have done a lot of business coaching over the years, and this is THE BEST that I have ever received. Shift has all the little secrets to propel you forward!

Louise Kershaw
Naturopath and Mother of 3
Loxton, Australia
www.riverlandnaturalhealth.com.au

Product Creation/Manufacturing

Product creation takes many shapes across boundless industries. You can make products like an iPhone, a box of Kellogg's Corn Flakes, and a stick of Dove deodorant. But in terms of the speaking business, the most common and best products are information-based products, like this book.

Products are created in all sorts of ways, but as a speaker you can capture and repurpose a program that you presented live just by recording it. I've done events where I've hired a camera crew, recorded my presentation, edited it and then made it into a full DVD set. That means no studio time or miscellaneous expenses. It's a fast, affordable and efficient way to create a quality product. Even if you do it in the comfort of your own home as a webinar or teleseminar, creating a product through speaking just makes sense.

Product Delivery

If you've created a product, marketed it and sold it, you need to have a way of getting it into the hands of the people who bought it. With speaking, most people will sell a seminar to a client, and then they will deliver that seminar. *They treat the seminar itself as a product.*

I encourage you to start that way because at the very least you can start delivering your product to a group, rather than one-to-one. But by the end of the book, you will see that every seminar has much more potential than just product delivery.

My invitation to you is to start thinking about every speaking gig as an opportunity to fulfill more than one of the above five needs in your business. Remember, the great gift of speaking is leverage.

Hopefully, you can now see how speaking meets the core components for success in business. Whatever industry you're in currently, you can increase your profits through speaking. But in order to do that, there are two skills that you need to master:

1. **An Effective Presentation** – a presentation that inspires action, as opposed to just a good talk
2. **The Elegant Business Model** – a business model that is not limited by your time, and frees you from the time for money trap.

You are going to learn how to effectively integrate these two concepts into your business – and the best thing is, they will work to enhance your business even before you step onto a stage.

BLUEPRINT IN ACTION SNAPSHOT

Recently I commenced "Rookie Developer" to help people through their first property development simply, safely and successfully. With the help of the team at Shift we've created our Elegant Business Model. We also ran two simple webinars attended by over 60 and 80 people. From those webinars, we were able to fill a room with 38 people for our very first one-day event.

Twenty-one of those 38 bought into our three-day event for $1,000 – that's nearly 60%!

It was really fun from the front of the stage to watch my very first run to the back of the room. It gave me a lot of confidence as I'd always had a lot of issues with selling from stage. The future is looking great. And a huge thank you to the Shift team. We couldn't have done it without you!

Troy Harris
Property Developer & Speaker
Dad of two gorgeous girls
www.RookieDeveloper.com.au

I know that my greatest value personally is on the platform or doing teleseminars or webinars. Any time I'm chatting away, I know that it's a revenue-generating activity for me. And I know that by the end of this book, you'll be thinking exactly the same way! But first we need to have a word about...

CONFIDENCE

Being a great speaker is all about being able to create emotional states in your audience. You might have heard this quote before from best selling author, Maya Angelou: "I've learned that people will forget what you said, people will forget what you did, but people will never forget how you made them feel." You can be talking about personal development, wealth creation, healthy living or French fries; no matter what, how you make people feel is what they remember. When you take on the identity of a speaker, you are better able to serve your clients, customers or family members in an incredible way.

You may be thinking, "I don't know if I'm confident enough to do that. I don't know if I've got it in me."

I want you to know that I haven't always been as confident as I am now, and in some situations I'm still rather shy. Actually, it's quite funny really. If you invite me to your place for dinner with a bunch of other people I don't know, I'll be the quiet one in the corner! It's only when I'm given center stage that I can be who I am. But usually I'm pretty shy. And it comes from when I was a child.

I was very timid as a kid. In fact, I wouldn't answer the telephone when it rang at home. I would push my little sister to answer the phone in case it was someone I knew. I felt that someone I knew was infinitely worse than someone I didn't know because there was a potential for embarrassment. But when I was in the sixth grade, I had a teacher who saw something in me that I certainly didn't see in myself. This teacher looked into my spirit and decided to cast me in the lead role of the school play. I was terrified.

We were acting out the Banjo Patterson poem, *Mulga Bill's Bicycle*. I was Mulga Bill, but fortunately, my character did not have to speak; I had no lines. All I had to do was bob up and down on my bicycle and fall off at the appropriate time. That experience sparked something in me, which, as I mentioned earlier, was the reason I went to drama school. Isn't it interesting how references from our past can play such an important part in our future?

I've come from shyness to creating massive results through speaking. So the good news is, it doesn't matter if you don't have confidence right now. I've had a number of students who started out apprehensive and uncertain, but later replicated very similar outcomes. I will introduce you to a few of them throughout the book so you can see that people from all different areas and with varying topics and backgrounds can make a great deal of money.

What I know for sure is that if I wasn't doing what I loved, I have no doubt I would be broke. As a speaker, you have to love what you're doing. You can't hide behind anything; you must be authentic. If you don't love what you're doing, people will see straight through you and they won't trust you.

Thankfully, speaking allows me to be my true self, connect with people all over the world, and share my tools for creating a lifestyle-centric business through my company,

Shift Lifestyle. Not bad for a young girl who was afraid to answer the phone!

> **OPPORTUNITY:** If this hits a nerve with you – if you know speaking is the way forward – I invite you to join me on a webinar (online training) to discover the secrets to a 7 Figure Speaking System. You can register for the next webinar at www.presentationprofits-blueprint.com/nextstep.

MONETIZING YOUR GIFTS

You may have picked up this book because you are not yet getting the kind of financial results you feel you deserve. You're working hard right? I believe my mission is to get you to a place where you are being magnificently rewarded for your passions and innate talents. I believe that if you were taken care of financially, you would give back, contribute and make a difference on a global level.

So let me tell you this: I may be successful now, but there was a time right after medical school that things were not so great for me. I was following my heart, which made me happy, but my bank account was another story. I had a debt of $19,000, mostly from the fees of the personal development seminars I had attended. Although I had started coaching and was doing what I loved, it took a long time before I started making any real money from it.

I remember one night, after receiving a phone bill that I couldn't pay, I was in tears talking to my mum on the phone, and it dawned on me the impact that my lack of financial security was having on her. I decided that night to make it work, not for me anymore, but for her; to repay her for all of the risks she took and all of the good things she created for me over the years. It was a shift from focusing on myself to focusing on contribution.

Now lets get clear about contribution. Some people, when they hear the word contribution, think you have to go and save the whales or save children in Africa. There's a perception that it has to be some grandiose act focused far from home. It doesn't.

For me, contribution started with my mum.

Shifting my focus was the first of two things I had to do to start monetizing and getting paid for my passion. I had done a lot of personal development work, but still did not have my focus in the right place. Turning my attention to my mum was a game changer.

After a few years of doing what I loved (coaching and speaking) and making some money doing it (imagine that!), I got to a place financially where I was able to give my mum a trip to Italy. She had been there just before I was born and it had been a lifelong dream of hers to go back. We went to Italy, just the two of us, and had a wonderful time. Giving back to her in that way was really powerful.

My family will always be an important driver for what I do, and now my husband and I have built enough wealth to ensure our parents and our kids will always be taken care of, we are able to contribute to other families around the world, too. I'm passionately committed to an organization called The Hunger Project (www.thp.org). The Hunger Project is a global, non-profit, strategic organization committed to the sustainable end of world hunger. They work in 11 countries in Africa, South Asia and Latin America to develop effective, bottom-up strategies to end hunger and poverty. The thing I love about this organization is the focus on shifting mindset first, and then investing in solutions in a holistic manner for the communities.

The point I'm trying to make here is this: while you're focused on trying to make more money to have more money, you'll never increase your wealth. When I changed my focus from acquiring money to contribution. Things started to shift dramatically.

But there was a second part to the puzzle. You see, when I wasn't getting the results I wanted with my speaking, I realized I had a choice in how I viewed my situation. My first option was to see myself as destined for failure – while everyone else on the planet could make money, I was obviously genetically incapable of it. My second option was to heed the words of a very wise man named Albert Einstein: "The significant problems we have cannot be solved at the same level of thinking with which we created them."

I chose option two! If I wanted to solve this money problem, I had to change the way I was thinking. At that point, I had been in studying personal development to within an inch of my life, but I wasn't getting the results I wanted. I thought, "What's missing? Come on. Let's take this to a new level."

It was then that I realized I had no system. I had no structure. I had a great mindset, but no vehicle or *system* for making money effectively! And I had to do something about it.

I discovered there are two types of people who are not getting results:

1. There are those who have access to all of the best systems in the world. They have been to Internet marketing seminars and real estate events. They know how to buy a house with only one dollar (just

joking – sort of). They have all of these systems in their arsenal that aren't working because their head is in the wrong place.

2. There are those who spend all of their money on personal development seminars and their head is totally in the right place – they could manifest a luxury car from thin air – but they're not making money on an ongoing basis because they don't have the system for generating cash flow.

You see, the thing is you need both. You need *the right mindset* and *a cash flow system.*

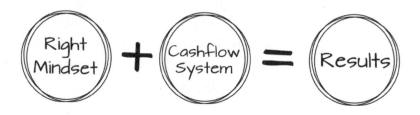

In this book we're going to concentrate on both shifting your mindset – making sure you're in the right place – and giving you the system and structure you need to get tangible results.

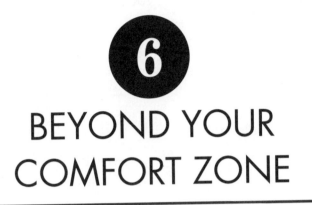

BEYOND YOUR COMFORT ZONE

Think about what you want to create through speaking. What are your goals? What is the driving force behind what you're doing? Remember, at first for me it was all about my mum.

ACTION
Clarify Your Goals

Put yourself in an environment where you feel connected with yourself and have the space to write. Maybe you like to sit outside surrounded by nature, or in your office with your music cranked high. Perhaps you prefer those quiet moments when you're lying in bed, right before you go to sleep. Wherever it is for you, I want you to go there when you have some uninterrupted time that you can dedicate to writing your goals. Use the space below or a journal dedicated to this process.

What do you want to achieve for:

Yourself

_____

_____

The people you love

_____

_____

Your community

_____

_____

People who do not have their own voice around the world

_____

_____

Get emotionally engaged in these goals. Write them using the language and the feeling that you would use if you are standing up on a stage and presenting them. Write them in a way that if you had to speak them, they would be exciting and inspiring.

BLUEPRINT IN ACTION SNAPSHOT

Within 48 hours of doing your workshop I went out and booked two workshops for myself: one in Sydney and one in Brisbane. I thought to myself, I've just got to do it after learning so many amazing things from you.

The first workshop we had 50 people, and made around $2,000, which was OK. The second workshop *we had 200 people and made A LOT MORE! So thanks to you I've got the courage to keep going, to keep doing it, and to get better and better at it. Thanks so much Joey for everything you taught me.*

Annette Welsford
Founder of the World's Largest online Style University
Brisbane, Australia
www.become-stylish.com

Once your goals are written, stand up, imagine you have a group of well wishers listening, and speak them. Say them loud and clear in a way you would if you had an excited, admiring audience in front of you. Say them with certainty. Say them with resolve. Repeat them over and over until there is no doubt in your mind that you can achieve them. (For those of you writing in bed, I know you're comfortable, but you're going to have to get up for this!)

Off you go, now. Have fun!

Welcome back. How does it feel to know what this journey is all about for you? Does it give you a sense of certainty, an inner strength that comes from being clear on the deeper meaning? If you're ever going to move others to take action through your speaking, you must be able to reach that place within yourself, first. Then you will have the ability to influence others.

You have to be the person who gets up, takes action and implements, right? If you don't do both of those things, you won't get the result. The main reason that most people don't take action or implement is because they're in a comfort zone. When we're in a comfort zone how do we feel? Comfortable. If you feel comfortable doing something, you say, "I'm in my comfort zone." Pretty straight forward.

The problem is that being in a state of comfort stops us from growing. Some activities that are typically outside of our comfort zone can be extreme activities like bungee jumping or scuba diving, or they can be as ordinary as speaking to strangers or using the phone (like me when I was younger). Now, I don't know about you but I don't much like being outside my comfort zone. Why would I? By definition it is uncomfortable!! So I like to think of *expanding* comfort zones rather than *stepping outside* comfort zones. I have always been an advocate of taking tiny risks, something I learned from Julia Cameron, author of the book, *The Artist's Way*. If you're not familiar with this book, it's a really fantastic read even if you're not an artist, because it's about creative *living*.

In regard to little risks, Julia talks about taking artist dates – fun, weekly, solo expeditions to explore something that interests you – with the intention of expanding your comfort zone. When I first read the book 14 years ago, I participated fully in the process and went on an artist date to a café that I had never gone to before, all alone. This act alone was a big deal for me back then, since I was a very shy girl.

While I was at the café I happened to overhear a conversation, ironically, about *The Artist's Way*. Here I was on my artist date and there are two people next to me talking about it! I thought to myself, "Okay God, I'm listening." So I got up the courage, walked over to these people and said, "Hi, I've read that book, too. It's awesome and I'm on an artist date right now."

I received a warm reception from them and we started to chat. They introduced me to some other people who then introduced me to the director of the local theatre company, who supported me in directing my first play. Everything was set in motion because of a little risk. It's a continual expansion. As you expand, something else automatically becomes comfortable and easy for you to do, and so then you expand again.

Now for you, speaking may be currently outside your comfort zone. Or speaking may be inside your comfort zone, but selling from stage is outside. Selling from stage may be inside your comfort zone, but hitting 30% conversions is outside. It doesn't matter what level you're at, because there's always another level to go to.

As your comfort zone expands, so does your definition of yourself. What could you do today to expand your comfort zone? I'm not suggesting you scare yourself senseless by doing things that totally make you quake in your boots; it's the little, tiny risks that can create the most exciting opportunities. So if you're feeling comfortable right now, it's time to expand yourself and commit to something new.

You may have a comfort zone when it comes to money. And I mean all things money. How you make it, how you save it, how you spend it, how much you think you deserve, how much you'll splurge on shoes – the list goes on and on. I want you to expand your comfort zone around money, so you'll be open to making more of it and sharing it freely. Les Brown, who I believe is one of the godfathers of public speaking, once said, "They tell you that money is not important, but it's usually the people who have lots of money who are saying that." I couldn't agree more.

7

MONEY MINDSET

Your beliefs about money have everything to do with your success as a speaker. I really want to emphasize that speaking is about more than just talking on a stage. It's about being congruent in your thoughts, beliefs and actions so that you can influence your audience to improve their own lives. If you harbor any negative beliefs about your own potential, they will see it and feel it.

Money is a hot button for many people, and your beliefs towards money are usually the result of events from your past. Sometimes our beliefs can be empowering:

- "The universe always provides."
- "I can be, do or have anything that I want."
- "Wealthy people are generous and contribute freely."

While other times, our beliefs are limiting:

- "There's never enough to go around."
- "I'll never be able to do that."
- "I can't have it all."
- "Wealthy people are greedy."

Do those limiting beliefs sound like they will bring happiness and fulfillment? I don't think so.

Empowering beliefs lift you up and support you in achieving your goals. Limiting beliefs don't serve you and may actually be holding you back. Your experience of reality right now is aligned with what you believe is and isn't possible.

Say a young girl is brought up in a wealthy family where money is never an issue. She'll grow up believing there is always enough money because that has been her reality. Another girl may grow up in a family where everything is a struggle and they have to scrimp and save. This young girl will grow up with the belief that there is never enough money because that has been her reality.

Each belief is the truth to the individual girl. With beliefs there is always an exact opposite that someone else believes because of the reality of their past. Another way to think of it is like this: first comes the belief, and then comes the reality. Or as author and speaker, Wayne Dyer, says, "First you believe it, then you see it."

The challenge is that we can have the best of intentions, but our limiting beliefs will sabotage us every time. The only way to fully realize your dreams – with speaking or with anything else in life – is to free yourself from the beliefs of your past and create a new and empowering way of thinking to take you into the future. So how do you do that? Well, you begin by paying attention to your internal dialogue and identifying the negative beliefs about money that creep into your mind on a daily basis. You know, the little voice in your head that tells you that you can't do it, you won't succeed, you're not worth it.

ACTION
Choose Empowering Beliefs About Money

Over the next few days, as you become more aware of what you're telling yourself, you may notice there is one limiting money belief that shows up more than others. It may be your 'go to' reason for not taking action. When you're clear on what that is, I'd like you to answer the following questions about this belief. Be honest with yourself and you'll be amazed at what you discover.

What is your most powerful limiting belief about money?

_____

_____

How has this belief affected your life?

_____

_____

In what ways is this belief *not* true?

_____

_____

How would your life be different without this belief?

_____

_____

What is a new belief that you can consider instead?

_____

_____

How will your life improve with this new belief?

_____

_____

In what ways is this belief true?

_____

_____

What can you accomplish with this new belief?

_____

_____

While we're on the subject of money, you have a responsibility as a speaker to deliver quality, passion and truth. Don't even get me started on the number of speakers out there who tout messages of spirituality, health, wealth creation and communication and have lives riddled with neglected relationships, bad health, average finances and poorly run companies. I'm not pretending for a second that anyone is perfect, but we can all strive to be living examples of whatever it is we say from stage. If you're an accountant speaking about accounting, have your books in order; if you're a doctor speaking about health, have a regular exercise regime; if you're a financial planner selling funds, have some passive income yourself.

Creating a lifestyle through speaking begins and ends with you. I am now an established expert in my field because I never settled with just trying. I've always been committed to excellence, and it's because of that standard that I've achieved a seven-figure business. I've traveled the world and met some incredible people, including experts, authors and multimillionaires who I now count among my personal friends and mastermind colleagues. I have an amazing relationship with my husband, Greg. Everything that I've created in my life is because of my commitment to excellence.

Today, what I used to make per year as a doctor, I make selling just one product (we now have at least two dozen!). That money comes in every month, forever, with no effort from me at all. Not even any speaking! The secret is ongoing monthly subscriptions, but we'll talk more about that as we get further into the book. When I do run an event, we usually make $500,000 to $1 million in sales, much of which we receive upfront. This type of income really gives us the opportunity to have some fun.

I hope you'll agree it's clear that I love what I do – and all of this joy is possible for you, too. I'm thrilled when I get to conceptualize a new project, design a presentation, deliver a talk or mentor a client. I get to work closely with my partner in life as well as business, and we have the opportunity to make a huge difference together. I'm living my dream and I want the same for you. So without further ado, I present to you *The Seven Profit Principles* you must master to make massive, leveraged income from your passion through speaking.

PART
TWO

THE SEVEN PROFIT PRINCIPLES YOU MUST MASTER TO MAKE MASSIVE, LEVERAGED INCOME FROM YOUR PASSION THROUGH SPEAKING

THE SEVEN PROFIT PRINCIPLES

After analyzing hundreds of speakers' businesses, as well as bricks and mortar businesses that have speaking as a fundamental part of their marketing, I have discovered there are seven key commonalities that make the difference between a profitable business and a part-time, attention consuming headache.

They are outlined in the following chart:

- **Passion**: Care about your topic and what it is you speak about.
- **People**: Find a niche of people who are as obsessed with your topic as you are and who have money to spend.
- **Promise**: Have a unique core promise of your business that sums up the problem your clients face and the way you solve it.
- **Propagate**: Effectively build your community and your profile online, offline and in the media.
- **Products**: Create products and services (preferably, though, not exclusively information prod-

ucts) with high profit margins that free up your time, i.e., your Elegant Business Model.

- **Presentation**: Have at least one solid Effective Presentation that results in your audience taking action.
- **Profit**: Automate and systemize your business effectively, through the right staff, software, business structure and legal setups to maximize your product for minimum energy and attention.

In this blueprint we will break down each principle in reference to:

- What it means
- How to apply it to your business
- How to avoid the pitfalls
- What action steps to take.

Are you ready to build the ultimate lifestyle business through speaking? Then let's get to it!

PROFIT PRINCIPLE ONE: PASSION

Passion and Why It is Non-Negotiable for a Speaker

Perhaps the biggest marketing myth expounded by marketers around the world is if you want to succeed in business, you must think market first, product second. They say find the best niche and solve their problem, whether you truly care about it or not. With speaking, it's the exact opposite.

As a speaker, you must care about your topic. You have to be able to talk about it until you're blue in the face. You have to believe in your products and services. You have to love them. You have to be willing to defend them to the death.

If you're selling vitamins online and you don't care about vitamins or health in general, you can still make money as long as your copywriting is good. However, if you're speaking about it, your personality and your passion (or lack thereof) shines through, so if you don't care, you're never going to engage anyone. Get the idea?

Your passion for your topic will connect you to your audience. Your passion for communicating your message will make your sales. Your passion for people will build your community.

BLUEPRINT IN ACTION SNAPSHOT

Before working with Shift I was working as a GP, and I was very good at it, but I knew I wanted to make a bigger difference. I secretly wanted to be a speaker of relationships and love!

After the Business Transformation Session, I decided to go for it. Since then I have been on the Channel 7 Morning Show once, then twice, and now with regular appearances – as the Love Physician, which has allowed me to get my message out in a more meaningful way. Thanks so much to the Shift team – I now have confidence to trust my passion, follow my dreams and live my difference.

Dr Angela Nguyen
The Love Physician
Sydney, Australia
Website: You can find
The Love Physician on Facebook

Many people think that passion is routed in love, but it can also be fueled by a negative emotion like hate. You can hate with a passion as well as love with a passion. How does this affect you? Well, it means that you can be just as dedicated to your topic if you see a sense of injustice. For me, one of the reasons I started Shift Speaker Training in the early days was because the seminar industry was getting a tarnished reputation due to the people on stage with less than exemplary track records and ethical structures. I was very passionate about introducing people to my views on speaking and helping them create profitable and sustainable businesses.

You may feel driven to speak on the platform because of a stirring inside of you that you can't ignore. You may feel that you must get your message out to the world. It's a compelling push from within you that you've got nothing to do with, and sometimes it's tough, right? But you get up and you do it anyway.

Now don't get me wrong here – passion doesn't have to look entirely emotional. You see, my husband, Greg, is not an overtly emotional person. Everything I am, he's the opposite. We're the perfect yin-yang, so for all of my emotion, he's all of the intellect. He used to tell me he wasn't passionate about anything and it was very troubling to him.

I believed him too, for a while. Until I tried to interrupt him for dinner one night when he was on Google searching for something. No matter how many times I called for him to come eat, he kept saying, "In a minute." He was utterly absorbed in what he was doing.

Now, even if you're more intellectually than emotionally oriented, I bet there is something that intrigues and fascinates you to the point that you can't be distracted from it – that compels your laser-sharp focus. If you thought about it, would you say that's true?

Greg loves Google because he loves learning. In fact, in our company if you want to know something, you don't Google it, you Greggle it! It's quite handy really, because no matter where we are when a question arises, he whips out his iPhone and says, "Just a second. I'll look it up." I would be very confident to say that Greg is passionate about learning and finding answers. But his passion finds expression through his intellect, not his emotions.

This is where so many people get tripped up. They're searching for that warm and fuzzy feeling, without realizing their intellectual fascination for something is an equally valid expression of passion. I'm very emotional, so "passion" is a word that juices me; but for Greg, he resonates more with the word "fascinated". If the word "passion" doesn't work for you, ask, "What am I fascinated by?"

As a speaker, you need to become skilled at tapping into what moves you mentally, physically, spiritually and emotionally, and communicating that to others. Even if what you're teaching is an intellectual concept like finance, you still need to access your passion/fascination to connect with your audience and move them to where you want them to go. It's from that place that you'll be successful and where you'll make a profit. So now let's get you clear on your passion/fascination.

BLUEPRINT IN ACTION SNAPSHOT

I'm on a roll now. I've been working with clients as a hypnotherapist for the last seven years and I've seen over 1000 clients one-to-one. But when I saw you up on stage I thought, "I want some of that."

I wasn't sure if I could do what I do, which is zone in on an individual, in the group environment. But I thought it was a lifestyle that I fancied. And it meant I could help more people quicker.

So it was something I had to go for. And I couldn't mess about; I'm at an age where I couldn't say I'll do it next year, or in five years. So I've just got on and done it.

I started out with "Motivation to Exercise", my introductory talk, and from that people came to my "Get Slim, Stay Slim" workshop. I'm now running my first retreat. So it's all happening on a roll, and I can't wait to get on and help more people and keep improving that bank balance. I'm really very happy.

Diana Powley
Hypnotherapist
London, UK
www.dianapowley.com

Know Your 'Why'

"What I do best is share my enthusiasm."
~ BILL GATES

"If you want to accomplish the goals of your life,
you have to begin with the spirit."
~ OPRAH WINFREY

"A business has to be involving, it has to be fun,
and it has to exercise your creative instincts."
~ RICHARD BRANSON

What do Richard Branson, Bill Gates and Oprah have in common, aside from making heaps of money of course? They all have a sincere passion for what they do. And their passion is shared by the consuming market, which is why they have such a global impact.

Passion is as vital to becoming an inspired entrepreneur as it is to being an inspired leader, such as Martin Luther King Jr. or Nelson Mandela. These are men whose speeches have stimulated action and changed nations. These are men who were really clear on their 'Big Why' – why they've simply *had to* share their message.

As for me, I'm not just teaching speaker training; I'm sharing my Big Why. And my Big Why is *Love*. I want you to be able to do what you love, with whom you love, and love every minute of it!

ACTION
Identify Your Big Why

Your Big Why is different from the goals that you've already written. Your goals are the specifics of what you want to accomplish and by when. Your goals include people, places and things. Your Big Why is more abstract and is just one word that sums up the feeling you want to give to the people in your world.

What do you wish for everyone in your world? Write down all the words that come to mind (e.g. love, fun, joy, abundance, understanding, compassion, freedom, connection, creativity, fulfillment, enlightenment):

_____

_____

_____

When you're satisfied with your list, circle the word that most makes your heart soar (or fills you with enthusiasm).

You may feel conflicted when looking at your words. You may think, "I want to give all of these gifts to everyone in my world! I can't choose one!" So let me help you simplify it here.

I did this exercise at a seminar, and a woman stood up who could not choose between positivity, optimism and financial freedom. I asked her what her real intention was behind those words. What did they all result in? She responded, "For people to be able to do what they want, with the people they want to do it with, by whatever means that's important to them." When I followed up with, "What's the word for *that*?" she quickly answered, "Freedom." If you're stuck on your word – or can't narrow it down to one – think about the similarities between your choices and ask yourself what is the result of all of those words? If someone had all those qualities what would they ultimately have? Then go with your gut reaction. Write it down here:

The reason why I work is to share _____ **with everyone in the world.**

Now, I'm not suggesting you go out and speak about Freedom or Love or whatever your Big Why may be, but to ground your message in the energy of it. Your connection to your Big Why will ensure you are able to sell and make money from the stage consistently. If you come from the energy of the word you just wrote down, your audience will never perceive you as pushy or manipulative. You can't be pushy and share Freedom at the same time! You can't be manipulative when you come from a place of pure Love!

When you come from the place of your Big Why, people don't remember the sale; they remember the experience and what they learned. I have the same intention every time I speak and in fact, before I even step on the stage, I get myself grounded in my Big Why. I send a funnel into the sky and I invite all of the good energy from above and below. Then I say a little prayer: "Dear God, please let me say whatever it is I need to say so they get what they came here to get." I imagine my heart space opening up, connecting with the heart space of every single one of the people in the room, and down that connection, I send love because that's *my* Big Why.

The second you step on stage, before you even open your mouth, take a moment and set your intention. Really connect to your Big Why. You're not really speaking about real estate. You're not speaking about accounting. You're not speaking about any of these things. You're speaking to give the audience the gift of your Big Why. Imagine if that was the first energetic intention that you sent out to your audience every time you stepped onto the stage, and when you got to your close, you just reconnected with that intention. Would that be special?

I make a lot of money from stage because it's not about the sale. I'm committed to giving my audience enough information so they can make a decision. And I'm not attached to whether they say yes or no because what I'm really focused on is giving them the gift of my love. That's it.

"Your job is not to teach as a speaker. Your only job is to love them enough that they feel they can do anything."
~ WILLIAM MARTIN

BLUEPRINT IN ACTION SNAPSHOT

In our first 12 months of speaking we hit our 7 figure speaking goal within $50 -not bad for someone who had a massive fear of public speaking and never envisioned in a million years he would be a public speaker!

And to think now we present with some of the legendary speakers like Andrew and Daryl, with Mal Emery, with Pat Mesiti and we now invite well known speakers to speak on our own stage because we get such awesome audiences along to our events! So within a very short time our lives have changed dramatically through learning how to present - I still pinch myself when I am on stage and look out over our large audience of 200 or so who are there to learn off Liz and I our strategies for buying and selling businesses and the fact that I am so confident and relaxed these days on stage absolutely amazes me.

So thanks Jo for providing such excellent speaker training at that 3 day event of yours - before every event or especially when we are writing a new workshop we still pull out the presentation profits manual to check over everything.

Matt and Liz Raad
Buying and Selling Business Experts
www.mattandlizraad.com
www.facebook.com/mattandlizraad

Love Your Topic

All right, the first part of passion is to know your Big Why, but as I said earlier, you've got to love your topic. You may already know your topic and hopefully feel a bit reenergized about it now that you've clarified the deeper meaning behind it. If you don't have your topic yet, knowing your Big Why is a great advantage. As you begin discerning possible topics, ask yourself, "Will this topic bring people _____ [insert your Big Why]?" If it does, you're getting somewhere. If it doesn't, move on to the next.

Let's have a little fun and look at some examples of topics that are making some of my students money. I know a lovely couple who are relationship coaches and they teach you how to find your soul mate. Their Big Why is Love and Connection. A travel agent who specializes in winery tours all over the world has a Big Why of Adventure. A personal trainer who speaks on how to get the most out of your body has a Big Why of Strength. A property manager's Big Why is Empowerment and her topic is real estate development. A beekeeper has a Big Why of Health and his topic is the benefits of honey. You can really speak and make money on any topic, can't you?

Are you clear on how your topic is different from your why?

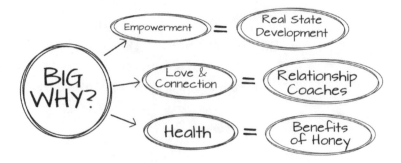

Here are some examples of how past Shift Speaker Training students have found their Big Why, related it to their topic, and grown their business. Feel free to have a look at their websites and see how it's all come together:

Name	Business	Big Why	Speaking Topic	Website
Ash Zuberi	Easy Living Property	Peace	Property Investing	www. easylivingproperty.com
Michelle Holmes	Mrs Whizzypop Social Media	Love	Relationship Marketing	www.mrswhizzypop.com
Caroline Nettle	Toxin Free Today	Health	Detox Without Drama	www.toxinfreetoday. com
Matthew Hill	Hill Networks Intercultural Leadership	Confidence	Building a Leadership Mindset	www.hillnetworks.com
Glenys Crawford	Crawford Kaye Business Growth	Freedom	Franchise Systems	www.ckbusinessgrowth. com.au

Your topic should be in line with your Big Why and you should be crazy passionate about both of them.

OPPORTUNITY: If you're passionate about your topic, then it's likely that there are millions of other people around the world who are passionate about it, too. All you need for a multimillion-dollar business is a few thousand of these people.

Determining your topic is a big deal and you may be torn between a few of them. I encourage you to narrow your focus to one distinct topic and take it from there. There is always time to expand your brand once you've established yourself. I discuss this process more in depth in our live webinars (www.presentationprofitsblueprint.com/nextstep), but I'm mentioning it to you now because it's so important. Some topics are going to be more profitable than others, so make sure to factor in the moneymaking potential of each one and choose your starting point wisely.

To help you along, here is a series of questions to pinpoint your true passion and the topic that was made just for you. Even if you already think you have your passion, answering the questions will help you refine it and may give you a fresh perspective or new insight.

ACTION
Self Reflection and Passion Hunting

Sit in a comfortable spot and speed-write (write without judgment or censorship) your answers to the following questions. Don't worry if you repeat some answers. If you do, it may actually support you in identifying patterns and getting closer to what it is you're meant to do.

What do you love to do? Write a list of 60 things. Don't stop until you have 60.

1. _____
2. _____
3. _____
4. _____
5. _____
6. _____
7. _____
8. _____
9. _____
10. _____
11. _____
12. _____

13. _____   37. _____
14. _____   38. _____
15. _____   39. _____
16. _____   40. _____
17. _____   41. _____
18. _____   42. _____
19. _____   43. _____
20. _____   44. _____
21. _____   45. _____
22. _____   46. _____
23. _____   47. _____
24. _____   48. _____
25. _____   49. _____
26. _____   50. _____
27. _____   51. _____
28. _____   52. _____
29. _____   53. _____
30. _____   54. _____
31. _____   55. _____
32. _____   56. _____
33. _____   57. _____
34. _____   58. _____
35. _____   59. _____
36. _____   60. _____

What are you good at? (*Yes, you are good at many things!*)
Write a list of 30 things.

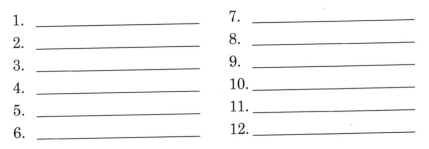

1. _____   7. _____
2. _____   8. _____
3. _____   9. _____
4. _____   10. _____
5. _____   11. _____
6. _____   12. _____

13. _____   22. _____
14. _____   23. _____
15. _____   24. _____
16. _____   25. _____
17. _____   26. _____
18. _____   27. _____
19. _____   28. _____
20. _____   29. _____
21. _____   30. _____

What do people compliment you on, or tell you that you do well?

_____

_____

_____

_____

_____

_____

_____

What fascinates you? What intrigues you?

_____

_____

_____

_____

_____

_____

_____

What do your friends and family complain that you "never shut up about"?

_____

_____

_____

_____

_____

_____

_____

_____

Where do you see the greatest injustice in the world? What really annoys you?

_____

_____

_____

_____

_____

_____

What topics do you constantly search for online or research in libraries?

_____

_____

_____

_____

_____

_____

What could you tell people about every day without ever getting bored?

_____

_____

_____

_____

What do you know how to do that someone else woke up this morning not knowing how to do? *(I can guarantee you right now there are things you know how to do that you don't value, and it's because you do them well and you've always done them well and you don't realize you have a system for doing them that people would kill to know!)*

What do you wish for everyone in the world?

Your answers to these questions will serve as a starting point for you to develop your topic further. Don't worry if it's not perfect. During the foundational period of your business you will refine your topic over time with every presentation you do.

A word of advice here for you: Choose a tight, narrow topic.

Let me illustrate this with my own story. By now I hope you can tell my deepest passion and the true heart of my business is Lifestyle Design, which really falls under the broad topic of Personal Development – I want to teach people how to free themselves from their business so they can reclaim their lifestyle. However, I'm impatient. When I first started, I didn't want to wait three years to build up a profitable business; I wanted to have it yesterday. So I refined my topic (or narrowed my niche, which we will cover in the next section), to get my business moving quickly and efficiently. I put my attention and energy into Shift Speaker Training first because speaker training was what I was best known for.

Lifestyle Design definitely has a presence within my speaker training business and one day it will have it's own day in the sun. So my advice to you, should you wish to accept it, is to narrow your topic, and select a tight niche. Which brings us to the next section....

Warning! Passion without the right people will cause your business to fail. You must take Profit Principle Two into consideration before starting your speaking business.

PROFIT PRINCIPLE TWO: PEOPLE

Find People Who Share Your Passion and Are Willing to Pay

Now that you've ignited your passion (or passions), it's time to put on your conscious filtering cap and ask yourself, "Is there really a market for this information?"

Your greatest level of success from speaking occurs when your passion matches up with a group of people who are salivating at the opportunity to find out more about that very same passion. It's also going to accelerate quickly from a profit perspective when those people have money to spend.

You see, if no one is willing to pay for your information, products or services, then you don't have a business – you have a hobby. This is the number one mistake that many speakers make and the main reason they never earn a cent in the speaking industry. To avoid this pitfall, you want to identify your target market, also known as your niche. Your target market is a small, specific segment of the market that contains your customers. They are the people whose needs and wants can be filled with your product or service. If you're currently in business then you most likely have already identified and marketed to your niche (at least I hope so!). Even if you have, please read on, because the clearer you get about your niche, the more effective your presentations and marketing will be.

Before you start building a business around your passion, ask yourself these four simple questions:

1. Are other people interested in this topic?

Are people currently looking for information or services and products related to your topic? You won't get far as a speaker if people aren't as interested in your topic as you are! So how do you find out? Try these strategies:

Specialty Magazines: Visit one of the larger newsagents or bookshops in your area and check out the specialty magazines available. Most magazines make their money from advertising revenue. If there is a magazine on your topic that has been around for a while, it's a fair bet people are looking for information on your topic – and are willing to pay!

Google Keyword Tool: You can also research this question from the comfort of your own home...or couch. Go to Google and search for their keyword tool and get some great information for free. There you can see exactly how many people are using Google to search on a particular subject. It's at https://adwords.google.com/select/KeywordToolExternal

Social Media: Utilize social media to find and meet people who share your passion. The Internet is a fantastic vehicle for connecting with like-minded people from all over the world. Search for your topic on Facebook. See if it's trending on Twitter. Visit blogs and forums to get a feel for the kind of people who are attracted to your topic.

Make notes and record your findings so you can start to get a clear picture of the level of interest in your topic. (A word of caution: Even if you think you already know your niche, research it anyway to ensure you're putting your focus in the right place. This will save you a great deal of frustration down the road.)

Once you know how many people are interested in your topic, your next step is to identify what kind of people they are. From there, you can narrow your focus to the group of people that will best support your business long-term.

And, yes, it is important you narrow your focus! The question I hear most often is, "Can you go broad?" – meaning, can you cover a large demographic with your niche? It's a tricky question because theoretically you can do this successfully, but it takes more time, money and effort. Take world-renowned Peak Performance Strategist, Tony Robbins, for example. He teaches personal development to everyone and their mother; no one is left out. And he has a marketing budget of hundreds and thousands of dollars to match. But if you're familiar with his early work, even he started small, focusing on people with phobias. Starting with a small niche is what I recommend for you, too (at least until you have the mega bucks to compete for business with the big guys).

The same thing goes for having multiple niches. 'Market segmentation' as it's called is fine, but for a speaker it may be difficult to manage early on. My advice to you when starting out is don't try to be all things to all people. A scattergun approach won't get you any traction; having multiple topics and niches sends mixed messages to the marketplace. Commit to one topic and one niche until you generate leveraged income from it, and then expand your brand to keep yourself engaged and interested.

Remember, you want your niche to be an inch wide and a mile deep. That means it's very narrow, it's very specific, but there are lots of people in it. You may choose a niche such as service professionals, newlywed couples, new graduates or new business owners. The clearer your niche, the easier and cheaper it is to market to them.

ACTION
Define Your Target Market

Take a few moments to define the demographics of your target market by answering the following questions. It's okay if your niche is a best guess for now because any information you can delineate will help you get the most value out of this chapter.

How old are they?

_____

What is their annual income?

_____

How do they earn their income?

_____

Do they fit a particular group? (Single mother, empty nester, small business owner, divorcee, young unwed professional, etc.)

Now, you're on the way to describing your niche market! For example, "She's a 40-60-year old professional woman, dealing with menopause, who makes $100,000 year or is semi-retired or retired."

Finally, to powerfully and strategically optimize your business, be sure your niche resonates strongly with your passion. Makes sense, right? You want to care about your niche just like you care about your topic. For example, my niche for Shift Speaker Training is primarily "advice professionals" (speakers, consultants, accountants, naturopaths, coaches), between the ages of 25 to 55, with an average income of $30,000 – $100,000 a year when they first start with me (it's always higher when they finish, of course). A niche for an accountant may be small business owners, individual investors or corporate executives, between the ages of 30 to 60, with an average income of $50,000 – $200,000 a year.

2. Is your niche market spending money?

Are people buying services and products related to your topic? Are there companies that are selling something to the people in your niche that solve their problem in a different way? If there are people in your niche who are spending money on services or products related to your topic, then there is definitely the potential for you to make money. You never truly know until you make your first sale, but we can at least have some idea.

Let me explain this concept with an example.

Every time I run a workshop there is at least one woman in the audience who tells me she wants to teach personal development tools to single mothers because she's passionate about helping them. Single mothers do spend money, but whom do they spend it on? Their children, every time. They certainly don't spend money on their own personal development. Therefore, even though they are a good, targeted niche, they will be reluctant to spend money on your product. It's the same with recent college graduates and new business owners – they don't necessarily have much money in their pockets.

Now, doctors are an interesting bunch. I hear all the time that I should niche down and teach personal development to doctors, but being a doctor myself I know what most of them are like. They don't like to be told anything! (Right docs? We already know it all!) So I know that this group is unlikely to pay for personal development. Of course, there are always exceptions to the rule, but we want to base a business on rules, not exceptions.

On the flip side, at one of my seminars a woman stood up and said, "I can't make money from my passion. No one makes money from my passion. It's just not a profitable business, but I love it." Her passion was showing her dogs at dog shows. She shared how there is no money in dog shows, because even if you win you don't get cash, you get prizes. I asked her if she had ever won a dog show and when she told me she had won many of them, I knew there was a business in it for her. Do you know what it is? You got it; her topic is educating people on how to win dog shows! Her niche is all of the people who are obsessed with winning them. If you've seen the mocumentary, *Best in Show*, then you know what I'm talking about (if you haven't, you must – it's hilarious). People will definitely spend money in this niche.

Here's a clever one... I know a woman in Australia who speaks on honesty and trust. If she had come to me before she had a successful speaking business, I would have said, "You can't make any money with honesty and trust." But she does have a successful speaking business and it's because she goes directly to corporations. She leads with, "Wouldn't it be great to have the tools to tell if your new employees are honest and trustworthy?" That opening works like a charm. She's got her 'in', the employers want to hear more and she makes the sale. How does she do it? By finding the problem that her topic solves.

So let's think... What topics are people spending money on right now? Social Networking? Wealth Creation? Public Speaking? Yes, yes and definitely yes (you're reading this book, aren't you?). Who are the people that are buying in these areas? Small business owners, entrepreneurs, service providers and consultants, to name a few.

There are plenty of ways to determine whether your niche has money to spend:

- Do some market research on people you know personally that would be in your niche. Ask them, "If I sold a product that did "x", would you buy it and for how much?" Use your Facebook account to poll your friends on your ideas. Whenever I'm considering a new seminar, designing a product or looking for a headline for a sales letter, I look to Facebook. I even requested feedback on the title of my latest book. It went something like this: "Hi, I'm off to Paris tomorrow to write my book. What do you think of this title: *The Lifestyle Shift*

– From Frantic to Freedom in Five Easy Steps?" People are amazingly helpful. Within minutes I always receive constructive feedback that helps my business.

- Research whether other businesses are selling to your niche already. For instance, I believe personal development tools targeted for menopausal women would sell well, because we already know they are spending a lot of money on Hormone Replacement Therapy. The market is already there; we just need a novel way of solving their specific problem.

- Research whether people are advertising to your niche. This is a proxy measurement, as there are some silly advertisers out there who spend money even though they are not making any sales. But as a general rule you can assume that if people are advertising to a group, that group is buying the product. You can measure this easily on Google Keyword Tool.

It's not until you're speaking to the people in your niche that you'll find out if they're spending money on your topic. Of course, the only surefire way to know if someone is going to spend money on your product is to close a sale. That's why I love speaking as a way of testing your niche, because you can get up, do a talk and it costs you nothing. If they spend money, you know you're on the right topic.

3. Can you easily access your niche market?

Can you easily access the people in your niche who are spending money on your topic? The answer to this question is a vital factor in whether it will be easy or difficult to grow your speaking business. Speaking is generally a face-to-face kind of business (unless you do most of your speaking on a teleseminar, which we will talk about later). So groups that consistently gather together live are the easiest to target.

I love a niche that meets regularly in groups. Why? Because any time there is a group meeting regularly, they are often looking for someone to come along and inspire them. Trust me; when I started speaking I had the National Speakers Association on my list of ideal audiences. I was hesitant to contact them because I'd heard rumors they didn't like people who sold from stage. But somehow they heard about me first and tracked me down and asked me to speak at their monthly event. Even the National Speakers Association is looking for speakers! So don't discount yourself. Every group, organization or company is looking for someone to add value and inspiration to their members or employees.

EASY TO ACCESS	DIFFICULT TO ACCESS
Meet regularly Meet locally Meet in groups > 30 Have regular speakers	Don't meet face-to-face Meet virtually, if at all Are mixed in among other types of people in large groups

Examples of easy to access groups include:

- Business owners at Chambers of Commerce
- Women entrepreneurs at networking breakfasts

- Singles at speed-dating
- Health-minded types at expos
- Young couples at home renovation expos
- Real estate investors at investment clubs.

Easy to identify but difficult to get together groups include:

- Mothers (limited time)
- Teachers (have to get through gatekeepers)
- CEOs (short on time and hard to get through gatekeepers)
- Agoraphobics (obvious reasons!).

3. What if your niche market can't get together?

If the people in your niche do not come together regularly or it's not possible for them to get together in a room, consider a teleseminar – or webinar-based speaking business rather than a live speaking business. This format works if you've got a small but global niche that can't all meet together in a room. If it's a great niche and you don't want to let them go, focus on virtual delivery platforms. They're convenient for you and your niche.

BLUEPRINT IN ACTION SNAPSHOT

Despite, being recognised by the AFR & TV as a Top Market Timer in Forex, shares & commodities and Trusted Advisor & Coach to financial firms & professionals, my message was not getting through to the "man and woman in the street". So I could not help them. Yet this is my life's purpose - to make successful investors and traders.

Once I attended a Joanna Martin Seminar I was excited! Joanna (Joey) showed me how to structure and deliver message that would get through. I learnt that I was too content driven in my free webinars - I was giving away too much - profitable as it was for the attendees!

Using just a few of Joey's simple steps the average person can now see what I have to offer to make a real difference in their trading and investing. They now get me! And I can now help them like I do with my high end clients. Thanks to Joey Martin. Here's proof...

A couple of weeks after I did Joey's seminar I tested these strategies in a free webinar. Instead of getting no sales and no reward - at that first –"Joeyed UP" webinar I sold 17 people at $2,000 each. That's $34,000!

Then two weeks later I did another free webinar and sold 8 people at $2,000 in the space of half an hour! You do the maths - $50,000 for a small investment.

My business has grown much bigger than that. As a bonus I now command $50,000 for 6 months consulting with my high end clients - I communicate better on all levels. Thanks Joey.

David Hunt
Trusted Advisor to Great Investors and Traders
www.profithunters.com.au

4. Does your niche market NEED your information, or do they WANT it?

Do the people in your niche – the ones who are spending money on your topic and who you can easily access – need or *want* your information? This question will directly impact the success and ease of growing your speaking business.

Imagine your small child has an ear infection. It's really sore and she needs to take her medicine, but the medicine tastes horrible. If you gave her a choice of a strawberry milkshake and the cough medicine, which would she choose? Most two-year-olds would choose the milkshake, and not surprisingly most adults would choose it, too. We're all still that kid at heart who wants the strawberry milkshake, not the cough syrup, right? Why else do we buy a bigger plasma TV before paying to get the car serviced? The car needs a service, but we want the TV.

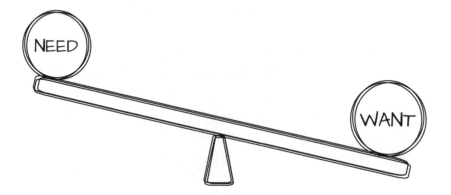

You will find it much easier to grow a speaking business quickly if you're speaking about something that people really WANT.

Does a doctor NEED to learn work-life balance? Absolutely! Do they WANT to? Nope, not usually unless they've just had a massive stroke, heart attack or other big wakeup call. Do they want a holiday? Yep! Create your speaking business around what your niche wants more than what they need.

And how do you find out what they want? You ask them. You get inside their heads.

BLUEPRINT IN ACTION SNAPSHOT

Before working with the Shift team, I was a coach, but I was confused on my niche and target. Through going through the program I've narrowed down my niche and it means that I can now present in a very engaging and simple way that gets me more clients every time I speak.

The confidence I have gained is incredible. The program is so simple to follow: a series of simple steps, one by one, and gradually delivering on outcomes which it makes it all achievable.

Sharon Styman
Business Coach
Tweed Heads, Australia
www.doubleyourbusiness.com.au

ACTION
Psychologically Profile Your Target Market

Make a list of 30 people in your target market, and survey them to find out their fears, frustrations, needs and wants. Ask:

What do they want?

_____

_____

What do they need?

_____

_____

What frustrates them?

_____

_____

What are they afraid of?

_____

_____

What keeps them awake at night?

_____

_____

If they had a magic wand, what would their ideal life be like?

_____

_____

What level of experience or education do they have on your topic?

_____

_____

What terms or jargon do they know and what will be new to them?

_____

_____

Care about your niche. Learn as much about them as you can so you can tailor your topic, product or service to meet their needs by giving them what they want.

If you start speaking – and selling – to a small, solid niche that loves your topic, has proven they spend money on it, are easy to access, and want and need your product or service, you will make money right away. In fact, join me on the live webinar and I'll show you how you could be making money in the next 30 days!

PROFIT PRINCIPLE THREE: PROMISE

Create a Compelling Promise to Your Niche That Captures Their Attention

You know those big, beautiful cathedrals that seem to be everywhere in Europe? Maybe you've been lucky enough to view them up close, but even if you've only seen them in pictures, you can't deny their magnificence. During a trip to Paris, I was only a three-minute walk from Basilique du Sacré-Cœur; the colossal church at the peak of the city. It's so perfect and enchanting. And it wasn't until the fourth day of walking past it that I looked really closely and noticed the one founding stone at the base (with an inscribed date of 1875) that was the beginning of the entire structure. In speaking, your promise is the founding stone of your whole business. Every product that you create, every presentation you design, and every opportunity you embrace is built on your promise.

In essence, your promise is your response to the problems or desires of your target market. It's the result of your journey up until this moment – everything that has created you, just as you are right now. It's formed and shaped by your speaking identity.

"What is this crazy lady talking about?" you may be thinking. I know it sounds confusing, but stay with me!

Let me first define your speaking identity and then it will all make sense. Speaking identity is something that, to my knowledge, no one else really teaches in the market-place. It's one of those things that I just went, "Ah, that's what it is." It just clicked.

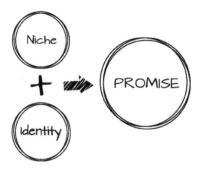

Your speaking identity is what makes you different from every other speaker on your topic.

Have you ever noticed how there are hundreds, if not thousands, of speakers in the following fields?

- Wealth Creation
- Real Estate Investing
- Stock Trading
- Personal Development
- Marketing
- Entrepreneurialism
- Relationships
- Leadership
- Spirituality.

And the list continues into infinity!

My estimate is that there are at least 100 'million-dollar-speakers' in each of these areas, too. So how do they all survive? Surely the world only needs one real estate mogul to teach property investing or one spiritual guru to bring everyone to enlightenment?

The reason the speaking world is big enough for all of these speakers on such similar topics is because every individual on the face of the planet has a unique identity. And it's every speaker's job to pick out their identity and promote it actively as their point of difference.

For a long time, traditional marketers have sworn by the golden rule that you must have a Unique Selling Point (USP) that sets you apart from your competition. I personally don't believe speakers have to obey (we're rebels, aren't we?).

Do you want to know the Joanna Martin rule? A speaker's identity *is* their unique selling point. Touché!

No one can be Deepak Chopra, but Deepak. No one can be Louise Hay, but Louise. No one can be Donald Trump, but Donald. Their USP is themselves. But when you read these names, what springs to mind for you? A brand. Every speaker, for better or for worse, has a brand. That brand is synonymous with their speaking identity. And if you don't take control of your speaking identity, the marketplace will take control of it for you.

So how do you create your speaking identity? It's made up of five different components, all of which influence and are influenced by the others. If you have all of them, you're going to have a really solid identity and you can guarantee that the marketplace won't be making up any stories about you. What the public knows about you will come from you, so that when they go out and talk about you to their friends, they'll be using your words, your language and your style. That's the ideal scenario.

If you only have a few of the components so far, that's fine, too. They're better than none. Don't wait to start speaking until you've got all five. Work towards having all five, but please start making money before then. Your identity is only going to be shaped as you meet your niche. This is a conversation that takes place between you and your niche. It's not a situation where you sit on the mountaintop, meditate for three years and then you finally come up with it. A working artist is someone who sits down and creates a little bit every day. It's the same for a speaker. It's the same for a businessperson. It's the same for an entrepreneur. The big idea doesn't come out of the sky. Don't wait for the big idea. Just get started because it's only when you're in conversation with your niche that the big idea will finally come to you.

I know that many of us would love to escape for a year and come back with a phenomenal promise and business plan. But the truth of the matter is if you go away for a year and come back with a business plan, it's not necessarily going to fly with your niche. And you're not going to know if it flies until you put it in the hands of your market. Why not make this a much more sensible, practical kind of journey, and do it one step after the other as you're in action, as you're making money?

So after all of that buildup, here are the five components of your speaking identity:

1. **Your Story** – Your unique accumulation of life experiences and the themes that it portrays

2. **Your Hook** – The one outstanding result you or one of your students has achieved that captures your audience's attention

3. **Your Angle** – The unique perspective you take on an old topic

4. **Your Title** – The self-chosen positioning you give yourself (sometimes this has been given by some-one else if you have been in business for a while)

5. **Your Brand** – The image, look and feel that you as a personality and all your collateral materials will portray.

These five factors interrelate in the following fashion:

The Five Components of Your Speaking Identity
The four external elements are created from the central element, your story.

Look at your personal life history and story through the lens of a curious outsider and you will be able to draw out the other four elements from there. You don't just decide out of the blue that you're going to take a new angle on a topic if you don't have the story to back it up. It's like saying, "Well, I'm going to teach marketing to chiropractors because chiropractors will pay for it," when you have absolutely no link in your story that connects you to them, or to marketing for that matter.

Your story is you. Become a master storyteller and tell your story like it's the greatest tale of all time. Then your hook, angle, title and brand will organically develop right before your eyes. It all comes back to your story.

Let's look at my speaking identity as an example.

My story tells of a young dissatisfied doctor whose favorite patient died, leaving her questioning the value of her work and the time she invested in it. She decided life was too short to waste valuable minutes in a career she loathed, so she resolved to follow her heart from that moment forward.

Every decision she made to follow her heart led her to greater and greater success emotionally, spiritually and financially. She grew from doctor, to actor, to coach, to internationally renowned speaker. (And on a side note, she can tell her story in 10 minutes, two minutes or 20 seconds – depending on what the setting requires.)

My hook is explaining how I took my own speaking business from zero to seven figures and two countries in 12 months.

My angle is a unique look at speaker training with a focus on the Elegant Business Model and Effective Presentations. That is, not just how to give a good talk, but how to **make a profit as a speaker.**

My title is the "Seminar Doctor" (although I don't promote it much).

My brand is cheeky, fun, wise, authentic and elegant. (By the way, I would never have called myself elegant, but people credit me with this all the time. Weird – but listen to your market!)

ACTION
Define The Five Components of Your Speaking Identity

1. Your Story: Write out the story of your life as though you are a master storyteller and your audience was made up only of your target market. (Or if you're not a writer, speak your story into a Dictaphone and have it transcribed.)

_____

_____

_____

2. Your Hook: What outstanding result have you or one of your clients achieved that you can help other people achieve? (Please note: If you or your clients have not achieved amazing results, you do not have to be the expert – you can be the interviewer of the experts. How do you decide if you're an interviewer or an expert? Ask yourself this: "Is *what I know* better than *who I know*?" If it is, you're an expert and you should have a good hook. If not, be the interviewer of experts. Oprah Winfrey is not the expert – she interviews all the experts, because who she knows is very impressive. You can do the same.)

_____

_____

_____

_____

_____

3. Your Angle: How can you approach things from a different perspective from everyone else?

_____

_____

_____

_____

_____

4. Your Title: What's something memorable and catchy for people to use to remember you that's related to you story or topic? For example:

- The Super Nanny
- The Horse Whisperer
- The Carpet Cleaning King
- The Career Oracle
- The King of Pop
- The Mentalist (had to include it – Simon Baker is from Tasmania!)

_____

_____

_____

_____

When choosing a title you don't want to be 'A' something, you want to be 'THE' something. Who is the number two talk show host in America? I don't know either. But who is the number one? If you answered Oprah you understand how important it is to be number one. Her show isn't even on the air anymore and people still consider her as the top! Choosing the right title will mean you're always in first place.

5. **Your Brand**: To determine your brand...

a) List 10 brands that you admire and why you admire them.

_____   _____

_____   _____

_____   _____

_____   _____

_____   _____

b) List your individual qualities that have received compliments.

_____   _____
_____   _____
_____   _____
_____   _____
_____   _____

c) Grab a stack of magazines, cut out images that appeal to you and paste them on a big poster board. Then, from your two lists and your poster board select the top three to five qualities for which you want to be known.

_____
_____
_____
_____
_____

d) Choose colors and images that support these qualities (these will be useful for when you create your collateral).

_____
_____
_____
_____
_____

e) Decide what you will wear in public at all times.

_____
_____
_____
_____
_____

f) List all of the elements of your brand – qualities, colors, images, etc.

_____   _____

_____   _____

_____   _____

_____   _____

_____   _____

When deciding on your wardrobe as a speaker, take these decisions seriously and be consistent. As a general rule you should be dressed up one tier higher than your audience, but it will depend on your brand. If your brand is 'Hawaiian shirts always', then make sure you always wear a Hawaiian shirt. If it's always a suit, make sure you're consistent.

Let me be perfectly clear (this is my stern teacher voice), just as it was important to discover your passion, choose your topic and identify your niche, it is also vital to clearly define your speaking identity. Remember, your speaking identity is at the heart of your promise, and your promise is the foundation of your entire business. Do the work now and enjoy the rewards of your efforts sooner than later. I strongly urge you to set aside some time – within the next few hours or days – to complete the questions and exercises for the five components. For more support and additional distinctions, join me on the webinar at www.presentationprofitsblueprint.com/nextstep.

Your Promise

Now that you've created your speaking identity, you can determine your promise. It will be a statement of who you are, what you do and how. It's the core reason your business exists. So the way to do it is to ask yourself, "What's the biggest problem my niche has, and how am I going to solve it?"

Just like an elevator pitch is a simple and quick summary of what you do, your promise should be delivered the same way, in less than 10 seconds. It should be conversational – not aggressive – and contain the following four points:

- Your Identity
- Your Niche
- The Biggest Problem of Your Niche
- How You and Your Topic as a Speaker Solve That Problem.

When assembling your promise, use words like:

- You know how...
- But...
- Well, what we do is...

For example, take a look at the promise of Shift Speaker Training:

"You know how **most speakers** are great at giving a speech, but are **struggling financially**? Well, what we do is show them how to **make over a million dollars** a year from their passion."

Practice writing and speaking your promise. There is no need to make bold claims or exaggerate what you can do. Be authentic, be real, and when it's the right one, it will feel natural and roll right off the tip of your tongue.

BLUEPRINT IN ACTION SNAPSHOT

I have done lots of presenter training courses and sometimes my brain gets caught up in all the tools and things I should be doing. Joey taught me to keep it simple and come from the heart. When you connect with an audience with authenticity, they listen!

So now I follow Joey's easy strategies and formats and I come from an authentic, fun place where I naturally exude enthusiasm and pull my presenter toolkit out as needed. I am so passionate about what I do and how it can benefit others. I now have the ability to let that shine through when I talk.

Eloise Ansell
Certified BodyTalk Practitioner
Flourishment.co.uk

ACTION
Create Your Promise

My Promise:

_____

_____

_____

Once you create your promise, pat yourself on the back because you have built the foundation of every product, presentation or promotion you will do from this moment forth.

PROFIT PRINCIPLE FOUR: PROPAGATE

Propagate Your Information and Become The Dominant Force in Your Market

Well done! We're a little more than halfway through the Blueprint and it's time for you to check in and be honest with yourself about your progress. Are you just reading along, thinking this is all very pleasant, and staying inside your comfort zone? Or are you pushing yourself and taking tiny risks? If you're feeling overwhelmed, remember: this process is about action and implementation. If getting results is what you want to do, then you need to adopt the mindset of a business owner. And a business owner is someone who recognizes they do not get paid for the time they spend being busy only doing what's comfortable for them. They get paid for the value they create in the world, a value that is made possible by expanding their comfort zone to include new things. That's really what it is.

So, hold onto that business owner mindset as we tackle the subject of dominating your market through propagation, or in other words, building an awesome community.

It's not the trainings you design, the talks you give, or even the products you sell that determine your success. It's the community of people who care about you and your information that matters most.

One of the biggest areas that speakers routinely fall short in is building their list of subscribers and raving fans. Great speakers are usually poor speakers financially because they neglect to build their community. I see this especially in the corporate arena, but it's the same in bricks and mortar businesses.

The time to think about building your community is before you even start a business. In fact, you've already done the groundwork on your community by researching the wants and needs of your niche. Do you see how everything you've completed so far has a stacking effect? Cool, isn't it!

You can take steps to build your community today. You don't even need to have a 'talk' prepared yet. Focus your attention on developing a warm, targeted list of people that are interested in you, whether they've purchased anything from you or not. When you cultivate a relationship with your non-buyers, they eventually become customers, too.

Four Reasons to Build a Warm, Targeted List

There are four main reasons why it's important to have a warm, targeted list of people in your speaking business.

1. Sales

As a speaker who wants to run workshops or trainings, having your own list of people is vital unless you want to do purely time-for-money corporate work. When filling your events, don't rely on joint ventures or other people's lists to fill your room. You need to have your own lead generation system that is not dependent on joint ventures. When I want to run an event, it's always my database who will form 60 – 70% of the people in there, then the rest is from joint ventures and promotions with other people's lists.

Even if you only plan on speaking at hosted events, you still want to grow your own community. These will be your clients and fans, the people who want to hear from you and buy from you.

BLUEPRINT IN ACTION SNAPSHOT

When we started basically from zero, we didn't have a list, we were organizing our own events and we were excited just to have three or five people coming. Now that we've built a community, we are so excited because we can organize an event in less than a week. We can easily get 20, 30 or even 40 people in a room who really want to be there and want to be learning about what we're sharing. They're asking, "How can I get my friends to come along?" It makes life so much easier with the great community we've created!

Jo Harrison
Melbourne, Australia

2. Product Launches

The key to a great launch of a new product is having your own list. Now whether that product is an event or a tangible information product that you're releasing online, once you've got your list, you've already got targeted people ready to purchase it.

3. Affiliate Programs

If you have a warm, targeted list, you can also make extra income through promoting other people's programs, services and products as an affiliate.

With marketing messages, make sure you're continuing to build relationships and rapport with your list and at the same time invite them to your seminar. The tone and format of your messages are more important than you may think. Share a fun lesson you learned this week (related to your seminar topic) that was so good you just had to tell them. Use the weekly tip format where you break down a success formula and send one step of the formula per contact message. My rule of thumb is to make your ratio of content to marketing information three-to-one.

> **Alert!** You never want your list to become jaded. Even worse, you never want to hear death bells as one-by-one people drop out of your list because ALL they ever receive from you is other people's stuff!

In the spirit of cooperation rather than competition, promoting other people's information and services to your clients can be a great fit. I have colleagues who are infinitely better at teaching their field of expertise than I am, and it makes sense to introduce them to my clients from time to time. But I am fiercely protective of my community and whom I introduce to them, and how often.

When deciding if you should you do affiliate promotions, first of all make sure you're doing it only for products, services or events that are valuable and interesting to your clients. If your niche is young IT professionals and your community is made up of techies, predominantly men, age 20 – 35, you wouldn't promote a raw food and holistic healing speaker. That wouldn't go over too well. If you're being promoted to someone else's database, confirm they're in your target market and your information is relevant to them, too.

As a side note, I know sometimes people get confused about privacy on this point. You're not asking the list owner to give you their list. This goes against their privacy act and is not standard practice. You're asking if you could be allowed to make an offer to their members, or better still if you could be introduced to their members as someone they endorse.

The strategies to market to your joint ventures and affiliates are similar to those you would use to market to your own list. You could ask them to:

- Send out a series of emails to their list, on your behalf, which sends the list to your website inviting them to register
- Allow you to post your sales letter directly to their members along with a call to take action to enroll in your seminar (you know, via snail mail – that old fashioned thing!)
- Invite their list to join your teleseminar/webinar, or allow you to become a guest on the list owner's teleseminar/webinar (the latter can work in your favor because the list owner has the relationship

with them, thus transferring rapport from the list owner to you).

4. Repeat Sales

Someone very wise once told me 70% of your sales come from past clients. That's why your list is so important. You can go back to your list time and time again. It's your community that already knows who you are and has an interest in what you do that will give you the highest repeat sales.

Don't just sell something to someone and then forget about them. Stay in touch with your clients. Always continue to give them value so they continue to trust you, enjoy what they've purchased from you and, more importantly, want to stay part of your community.

Four Qualities of a Good Community

There is a difference between a list or database and a community. I strive to build communities, not lists. Foster a relationship with your subscribers beyond just knowing their name and email address. Focus on building up your numbers, yes, but always nurture the relationship, too.

List $\times$ Relationship $=$ Community

1. Bigger Is Not Always Better.

We have a saying at Shift Speaker Training to beware of bright shiny objects – things that look sexy and attractive but distract you from the core functions of your business.

In this case, it's the false notion that you need a huge list for your business to succeed. It's far better to have a small, responsive targeted list rather than a large list of people you don't know. Ask yourself, "How can I create a warm, targeted list of my own?"

In speaking circles, you may often hear speakers boast about their large and impressive list or database. I will admit size is relevant, but it's only one piece of the puzzle. The other is, of course, the relationship that you have with that list. A quality list is a database of 1,000 people who love you, respond to you like a rock star and rave about you to all of their friends. If you have a huge list of 200,000 people from every walk of life, but they don't respond to your marketing, then the quality of that list is pretty low. Your list is where the security lies in your business so treat it like solid gold.

We made our first million dollars from a database size of less than 1000. So size certainly is not everything!

BLUEPRINT IN ACTION SNAPSHOT

Things sure have changed in my business thanks to your information, Jo. Here's a brief rundown of my last 2 seminars...

March 2009 – Booked a venue, organized catering, aimed for 50 people, didn't charge for it, 6 people turned up, all of them were friends who come along and support me each time, sold nothing, cost $500.

February 2010 [now] – Booked a venue, organized light refreshments, aimed for 40 people, charged $67, 38 people booked in to date, all of them paid, most of them I don't know, not enough room for my friends *(they're actually crewing for me), so far I'm ahead $500, bookings are still coming in, OMG!*

I followed everything you did in the How to Fill a Room manual and it worked! I had this overwhelming moment when I logged into my emails and in one day the payments just kept coming and coming. I remember thinking, "So, this is what Joey's been telling me."

I have covered my costs and am now just watching the profits come in. I honestly don't know how to thank you. I've been trying and trying to get this moving for a couple of years now, and for the first time ever my dream is just a couple of days away. My event is on Sunday.

Your generosity and care regarding my success is inspiring and you just make me want to step up and play a bigger game. But it's more than that – it's the fact that you really pull back the curtains and take me step by step through the how that makes all the difference. Thank you is truly not enough.

Jo Baker
Lifestyle Coach
Melbourne, Australia
www.believelifestylecentre.com.au

2. Responsiveness is Essential.

A small, responsive list is better than a big, unresponsive list. Always be growing only at the rate that you can continue to maintain a great level of responsiveness – on both ends. While you want to hear from your list, they want to know you're paying attention to them, too.

With automated customer service being so prevalent, we have become accustomed to punching a million numbers into the phone and wasting half of our day to speak to a real person, or sending an email out into cyberspace with barely a hope of ever hearing back. It can be frustrating and you feel like no one cares. Show your list that you are there for them by being in communication with them. It's communication that breeds community. It's contribution that breeds community. It's giving your clients some really valuable information and building a relationship with them. Don't be a pest to people. Be a resource. If they have a question, they can come to you and know they'll get an answer.

At Shift Speaker Training, we will send out an invite to a webinar and if people can't attend, they write back and tell us, "I'm so sorry I can't make that. Will it be recorded and can you let me know?" Our community shows us the courtesy of letting us know their plans, and we extend that same courtesy back to them by responding. They write because they know they will get an answer. *Every time.*

Social media, especially Facebook, is facilitating this sense of community even further. I feel I know people long before I actually meet them at an event!

3. They Must Be Interested in YOU and YOUR Information.

One of the things you'll notice with emails from me is that they often contain a little paragraph or a video about where in the world we are and what we're doing. With a format like this, your community gets to catch up with you on a regular basis to find out where you have been and what new things you can tell them to keep them in the loop.

Build a list of people who are interested in your material. It might be great that you just attended a social media seminar and met all of these influential Internet marketers, but beware of adding all of your new friends to your list if your speaking business is centered on financial professionals. Having 200 names and emails of random people who someday hope to speak on Internet marketing to their own niche won't serve your bottom line. I want to be really clear that you need to distinguish between someone who you're networking with and someone who's in your community. Just because you have their business card, does not mean they belong (or even want to be) on your list.

4. They Must Not Be Jaded.

Being on the receiving end of continual marketing is exhausting. Think about how you would feel if you were bombarded almost every day with *irrelevant* promotions from someone you thought you could trust. You would become frustrated and possibly unsubscribe from the list.

I believe there's no such thing as too many messages if they are full of free, valuable content that your community wants and needs. Strike a balance between invitations to action as well as providing quality information. Often people miss important emails about a free gift or a seminar coming up soon. You'll find that one email won't be enough to get action. In a promotion we did last year, we sent out eight emails about one single product that we were promoting. It was the sixth or seventh email where we got 70% of the people to take action. However, an influx of emails without valuable or interesting content will cause a problem. Keep a close eye on how many people are unsubscribing from your list and adjust your behavior accordingly.

Propagate Online and Offline, Increasing Your Celebrity Factor

If you are clear on your speaking identity and have a good idea of your ultimate community, get yourself out there!

1. Online Strategies

There are so many online strategies being used today, it's easy to build up your brand recognition utilizing the right ones. There is definitely no shortage of websites, programs and products available to teach even the least tech savvy person how to create a presence on the Internet. Anyone in their lounge room can become a web-celeb, as long as you have useful and interesting things to say.

Here are some simple tips to get you started:

1. Set up a blog using WordPress.org under your own domain name, so that when people hear you speak, they can easily search for you and find you online. If you're new to blogging, check out the great training videos that Yaro Starak and Gideon Shalwick give away on BecomeABlogger.com. If you want support with taking this a step further and creating a 'Pro-Speaker Hubsite', drop us a line and I'll introduce you to my personal Tech-xpert.

2. Use Facebook, Twitter and LinkedIn to announce your new articles and send people back to your blog.

3. Shoot some simple, content rich videos and host them on YouTube. You can post these on your blog, but always have a link to your website so if people are watching them on YouTube they can find you! (You don't have to hire a professional videographer. Just use a digital camera or a camcorder.)

BLUEPRINT IN ACTION SNAPSHOT

A whole new world instantly opened up for me – talk about overwhelm and excitement rolled into one! I am now taking it step by step, and loving it!

Before doing the webinar with you I was horribly frustrated and stuck, not knowing where and what to do to shift my business to the next level.

Since doing the webinar with you I have completely remodeled my website and I am continuing to add more as the days go by.

I have learnt so much about copywriting, calls to action, and opt-in boxes. I have got PayPal up and running now, and my finished Blueprint will be added to the opt-in box. I have used the word search and also sent out a survey through SurveyMonkey.com...it's all so exciting!

I now have links throughout my website and in my emails making it easy for people.

My CD's are lined up ready to go and I have begun to put my "Elegant Business" packages together. I have added a weekend away for two people to my coming seminar.

Your ideas are so simple and easy to put into action. You have given me structure and an easy system to follow. I have now begun sending out fortnightly newsletters.

I have begun attending women's groups and networking breakfasts and have signed up an extra four people for my next workshop just through using your copywriting tips in my emails. So I made my money back AND MORE in the first week!

Thank you, thank you, thank you!

My next challenge is going to be to set up a teleseminar or webinar and a blog...there is no stopping me now!!!

I will also be taking on a new staff member because of what I am now determined to achieve in my business.

Thank you, Joanna.Life has stepped up a notch for me now and the sky is the limit.

Deborah Bow
Azur is Perfect
Clinical Hypnotherapist
www.azur.com.au

2. Offline Strategies

As a speaker, it's also easy to build up your offline credibility, as there are always organizations looking for regular speakers on a variety of topics. It's just a case of getting yourself there, networking and getting known.

1. Speak anywhere and everywhere possible on your topic. Sell where you can, but if not, at least have a call to action at the end of your presentation for people to join your newsletter list.

2. Do regular press releases and get yourself known in the media. For some of the Shift Speaker Training members, their business took off after they appeared on TV, and getting booked is easier than you think.

3. Write a book ASAP. Being a published author always makes it easier to get on TV, as well as opens doors to other speaking opportunities.

These are just a selection of ways to start building your celebrity. Ultimately, you need to convert that awareness into building a community, so let's have a look at that now.

ACTION
Start Building Your Community Now

What is one strategy for building your strategy online that you will implement right away?

_____

_____

_____

What is one strategy for building your strategy offline that you will implement right away?

_____

_____

_____

The Five Keys to Building the Right Kind of Community

The number one question about communities that my students always ask me is, "Where do I start?" And what I always tell them is to give something for free in return for contact details. Give away anything that your target market is going to value, and after all the work you've done on identifying the wants and needs of your niche, that should be an easy task! The best thing you can give away is something that is easy to create and deliver.

Here are some of my favorites because there are no hard costs for production or shipping; they're all available electronically:

- Teleseminar
- Mp3
- Ebook
- Informative article
- Training module/video tutorial
- Free chapter of a new book (even a yet-to-be released book).

Imagine: You're running a wealth creation seminar in six months' time and you want to build your list so you can market to them around wealth creation. It may seem obvious, but make sure the topic of your free gift is related to wealth creation. If you make it about speaking or marketing or anything else, you won't attract the right people.

Whatever you give away in return for details must have a high-perceived value. It must also be relevant to the kind of list you want to build. Don't be afraid to give away your best stuff for free, because where your real value comes in is in helping people to implement it and get through the obstacles.

The following five keys will help you get focused on what to give away and the best way to do it.

1. Speak

If you're speaking in front of a live audience, ask the people in the room to hand in their business cards in order to receive the free gift. Make sure the gift is valuable to your audience and that you send it as soon as the gig is over. It could be something like an interview with your top four clients on how they succeeded using the strategies you use. You now have your own instant list!

Rakesh Kakaya 19 July at 00:42
Hi Joanna,

Thank you so much for your inspiration. I have finally done it. Firstly launched my optin page/ ebook and community builder. Secondly I started speaking. I had my first client appreciation night and Call to action was 1 referal from the 18 people that attended I have 12 referals worth £300.00 each...Yeah! Not a bad start. Would love to share the platform with you soon.

www.thoughtsbecomereality.co.uk

2. Blog

If you start a blog, as I mentioned earlier, you will automatically start to build a list. People can subscribe to be updated of posts of what you're up to, where you are and inside information that you can only get by subscribing to your blog. They can subscribe using their name and email address. What do they get for free? You're giving away your blog article delivered straight to their inbox.

3. Newsletter

We noticed our list started to boom when we commenced a regular weekly newsletter. It's great for building a list because people get value from it and if you produce good quality content, people will be hooked. You can include articles, videos and all sorts of material to keep your community interested and growing. You can also have an opt-in box for this on your blog too.

We have since tweaked our model and send regular articles and videos, but not a full-blown newsletter. We're testing that now. Always be open to trying new things and find what suits your community best. The key is to offer great value regularly!

4. Website

Make sure there's an opt-in box on your website. Either they're opting in to get free information or they're opting in to subscribe to the newsletter. We use a couple of different things depending on what the website is and what we're selling.

There are some secrets to creating useful opt-in that actually convert. It's beyond the scope of the book, but to see our opt-in websites that convert well, have a look at www.shiftspeakertraining.com/bookblueprint (this is a dedicated opt-in page), and www.shiftspeakertraining.com/bookblog.

5. Tell a Friend

Give your community the opportunity to tell a friend. This can be done at your speaking gigs. Also, use an opt-in box on your blog, newsletter or website. It can't get any easier than your community recommending you to people they know who will be interested in your information. Be sure to give a free gift as a reward for telling a friend.

ACTION
Design Your Free Gift

BLUEPRINT IN ACTION SNAPSHOT

Since training with Joanna, I have spoken at over 20 seminars and workshops (some of my own and some on other people's stages) creating an extra £100,000 from my speaking engagements alone, on top of the existing revenue from existing clients and other forms of business generation. For 2011, I am taking what I learned from Joanna and focusing more on speaking at bigger events around the world where I will be able to engage with bigger audiences to ultimately get more clients buying my products.

My first seminar had just seven people. Just a year later, I am speaking to audiences of 1,000 people on bigger stages internationally and speaking at corporate events for staff training on Internet Marketing strategies.

Suraj Sodha
Internet Marketer
InternetMarketingHighway.com

Keeping in mind the wants and needs of your niche, what free gift will you design to build (or strengthen) your community?

_____

_____

_____

Focus on one piece at a time, one day at a time. Don't expect market domination to happen overnight, but if you release regular content online (a couple of times per week) and you speak regularly, you should have a solid community within six months. The good part is that as you build your celebrity and credibility by propagating your message, you become front of mind for promoters and event planners who are looking for speakers.

> **TIP**: If you do a regular newsletter, always put a section called 'Need A Speaker' to promote that you are available to do presentations. I have received many referrals and inquiries this way!

PROFIT PRINCIPLE FIVE: PRODUCTS

Planning Your Elegant Business Model – A Suite of Targeted Products

Would you marry someone you had just met? The overwhelming number of people would say, "No, I need to get to know someone first."

Here's a typical scenario:

You meet someone. They seem nice, attractive and funny...

You have a coffee. They're not completely insane like the last one...

You go out for a drink. They like the same things you do...

You have dinner a few times. You share the same values...

You date exclusively. They support you and you like who you are around them...

You introduce the parents. They don't leave you...

You get engaged. This is the one...

You get married. It feels right.

Of course, there are a few mad-capped individuals who meet someone in Vegas, get swept away by the romance and get married that night. But for the most part, we like things to roll out a little at a time. Running a business is the same. You have to honor the human need to build trust, and allow people to get to know you as a person before making big commitments. In the speaking world I refer to this as your Elegant Business Model.

The Elegant Business Model

In a nutshell, the Elegant Business Model is the process of designing a product line to match the natural way in which an individual will develop loyalty. Just like the dating example outlined above, a new client will need to develop trust with you before they commit to spending lots of money with you. The ultimate outcome in a business sense is to become the trusted advisor of your clients. The Elegant Business Model describes how you can do just that.

As a quick illustration, the graph below shows how as a client develops a trusting relationship with you over time they will spend more with you:

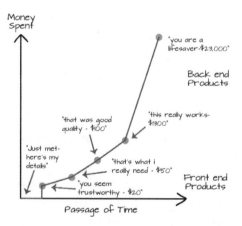

Before you fully understand this model and why you should employ it, we need to define trust. This is not the dictionary definition of trust, but in my experience is a watertight, functional definition that is very useful in the development of relationships.

It has two components:

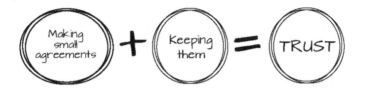

Under this definition, you can turn the esoteric notion of establishing trust into a practical step-by-step strategy you can employ in your business. Every time you make an agreement with someone, there follows the opportunity to either increase trust or decrease trust. If you fulfill your end of the agreement, trust levels go up.

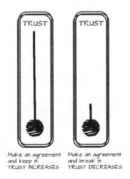

Make an agreement and keep it. TRUST INCREASES   Make an agreement and break it. TRUST DECREASES

In business, people are becoming cynical. They've heard it all before. They've been burned and let down. Salespeople have made promises they haven't kept. In general, the consensus has become "do not trust salespeople". Rather than fight this reality, accept it and then be free to create an incredible business model that will satisfy the decision-making processes of your clients.

By employing the Elegant Business Model in your business, you give people the opportunity to do business with you in direct proportion to the level of trust you have been able to generate. It gives you the ability to make and deliver on a small promise to a client in return for a small amount of money, thus increasing trust so that next time you can make a bigger promise for a bigger amount of money.

THE ELEGANT BUSINESS MODEL AT WORK: DAVID

David was a Life Coach, and a good one at that. He was trying to sell people into a 10-week, intensive, transformational coaching program. The price was a bargain (based on the results he was getting with clients) at just $3,200, but he rarely got a client. He would meet people through networking, join them for a coffee and try and close them on a $3,200 product. Tough gig.

Problem #1: The price point is too high compared to the level of trust.

Problem #2: The time commitment is too high compared to the level of trust.

ENTER THE ELEGANT BUSINESS MODEL

David got smart and re-structured his business. He started a blog to share his thoughts and some of his strategies for free. He created a newsletter that he gave away free every week in return for the name and contact details of people. His database of prospects began to grow. He invited his prospects along to an evening seminar for $27 where they were introduced to him and his style and they took home some value. At the seminar David sold an eight-week Teleseminar Coaching Program for $497 (note shorter time commitment, over the phone, lower price point). At the end of the Coaching Program David sold one-to-one Breakthrough Coaching, three sessions for $3,795 (note higher price point than previous for less work).

David's problem had been that he had no opportunity to develop trust with his potential clients before they spent a relatively large sum of money with him. Occasionally, he would come across someone who trusted him from the get-go and would spend the money, but more often than not he wouldn't.

By employing the Elegant Business Model, he was able to systemize the development of trust with his prospects so that even the most skeptical would be able to at least give him the opportunity to impress them.

ACTION
Reflect On Your Current Business Model

Currently, what is the first opportunity your clients have to do business with you?

_____

_____

_____

What response has this generated for you so far?

_____

_____

_____

How would you improve this first opportunity in line with David's example of the Elegant Business Model at work?

_____

_____

_____

Remember – Speaking is About Creating a Lifestyle

The added benefit of an Elegant Business Model is that you are creating *information products* which package up your knowledge, rather than trading your time for money. This is the secret to freeing up your time and creating the ultimate lifestyle business as a speaker.

The worst thing that happens to speakers is they succeed. It really is. Then they're flying here and there, speaking in Ireland this weekend, speaking in London next weekend and then flying over to Los Angeles, where they've got a radio show they need to do on Thursday night. Then they're speaking that Friday and Saturday, and on Sunday they wake up and although they've got millions of dollars, they have no life because they don't have an Elegant Business Model.

Most speakers think the backbone of their business is their seminars. They sell a workshop, which they then have to teach. At that workshop they sell another workshop, which they then have to teach. They go ahead and run that one, sell another and the cycle continues. And then they die. (No, they don't really die, but they're completely exhausted.) So the greatest problem for speakers is success. I want you all to succeed, but succeed elegantly.

At Shift Speaker Training, our goal is always to have our overheads covered by subscriptions to our membership sites. This is what I want for you. As part of a subscription, clients pay you an ongoing monthly fee for some service. It may be to be part of a select community where they receive content exclusive to them and whatever other benefits and perks you want to give them. Think about the subscriptions you already have. Maybe you get a magazine every month. Or your vitamins come right to your door, or your movies and DVDs.

Many subscriptions online are free – newsletters, videos, etc. That's all well and good, but what you want is higher-end subscription programs where you give heaps of value and your customers see the value and are willing to pay for it.

I believe you absolutely must have a subscription component to your speaking business. Every time I run a workshop, it's all profit. It's all ice cream. That's where I want you to get to because otherwise you end up like a little mouse on a wheel, chasing the next bit.

BLUEPRINT IN ACTION SNAPSHOT

Our business is called Practice Paradox and we teach accounting firms how to market and how to sell. Sure, well, prior to doing Presentation Profits Intensive, Jo, my business model was a pretty traditional one of consulting, selling time for money and I was flat chat working massive amount of hours. Some days [I was] literally getting up at 3:00AM to start my workday.

There was a couple of key pieces and content that you ran through that to me were profound. I remember you said, "Here are six ways of making money... let's start with the dumbest." And you wrote the first one up and I went, "Hey, that's me! Oh, congratulations, I'm on the dumb rung of the ladder." That got me thinking, "Yes, look, this is just not leveraged, selling my time for money, selling my time for money!"

When I got back from your three-day PPI course, my wife Isabella and I were sitting at the baggage carousel waiting for my bags to come out from the slide and she asked me, "So, what did you learn?"

I said, "Well, we're going to redesign our business and it's going to be a scalable business where I'm not just doing it one-on-one."And she said, "Really?"

I said yes and she started to cry. She said, "I just don't see a light at the end of this tunnel. You are working yourself into a grave here," and she was really emotional about it – we both were.

But your Elegant Business Model was really the genesis of me completely reinventing my business model so that now we can pick and choose when we do consulting. Our business model now has shifted to training and education, where 80% of it is delivered over the web and 20% of it is delivered through live workshops.

We now have a business that's completely scalable – whether we have 10, 20, 50 or 300 members in our membership site model, it's a similar amount of work for us and for me.

It's kind of funny to look back and think that when we launched Practice Paradox, which was two Februaries ago, I did a webinar, because I've done that a lot over the years and it was kind of like I was standing there with the little thimble, a tiny little cup of capacity, and then the webinar made it rain! And I thought, "Yes, I've got my three clients and the other 50 that want to work with us, well, you're going on a wait list!"– which was ridiculous. So now we can work with 50 clients at a time because we had that one-for-many educational model rather than just one-on-one.

In our first webinar of the new model we picked up $180,000 in sales. So now Isabella sees a bright light at the end of the tunnel. We know exactly where we're headed and it's really exciting for us and it's really exciting for our clients as well.

We can see that we have a business that is truly a business now, and consulting really is just a job with a fancy title on it. So, we really feel that we've got a vehicle that will build the lifestyle to enable us to enjoy the journey and spend time with each other and *our two young children. We've got 4-year-old Nelly and 7-year-old Ned, and if I'dkept doing what I was doing, I'd be one of these guys, and I've met them over the years – men and women who get to their 50s and 60s and say, "Oh, hang on, what happened to my children's childhood? I kind of missed that." So, as you could picture, that is the most valuable thing for us.*

Michael (MC) Carter
Consultant and Educator to Accountants
www.practiceparadox.com.au

So let's recap here. An Elegant Business Model is one which:

- Frees up your time
- Is systemized so you only have to make every effort once and then it keeps rewarding you over and over again
- Allows you to make a lot of money
- Mirrors the natural decision-making process of your clients.

If you want to have a life, you need to create an Elegant Business Model. Don't fall into the trap of only selling your time in workshops, trainings or one-on-one work. Make information products. And not just one – many! Ultimately you want to get to a point where you have something at a minimum of four different price points.

Here are some other examples of the Elegant Business Model at work:

- A business consultant offers a free business audit upfront.
- A drycleaner offers a free suit cleaning upfront.
- A beauty therapist offers a simple facial treatment for $65 before recommending microdermabrasion for $350.

I'm not saying that every speaking business should start with a free or even $20 price point. Try to buy something from Ferrari at that price; you'll be walking out empty handed. Your price points will be dependent on two main factors:

1. **Your Niche:** The more specialized, the more you can charge (to a point)

2. **Your Brand:** The more trusted your brand, the more you can charge (e.g. Ferrari is a trusted and sought after brand, hence the price point is high).

BLUEPRINT IN ACTION SNAPSHOT

I was able to get 73 people to my first seminar, of which 23% converted to the next stage of the Elegant Business Model.

And now we've got the next seminar, and the CDs, and everything is just working perfectly according to the 7-Figure Speaking System plan. I can't thank you enough!

Dr Maura McGill
Speaker
Sunshine Coast, Australia
www.DrMauraMcGill.com

Implementing an Elegant Business Model into Your Business

When designing products to give and sell to your clients, they have to be created for your clients and they must always fulfill the promise of your business (if you need to, review your promise from Principle Three). The best products are those your clients have told you they want. If you don't know, invite your current community to tell you what they want. Ask at events, on social media, in your newsletter and through SurveyMonkey.com (a really easy and affordable online service).

Alternatively, just use the Magic Wand Technique outlined here.

ACTION
Wave Your Magic Wand

1. Ask yourself (or your clients), "If time and money were no object, what would my target market want more than anything else in the world?" Brainstorm, free form, and write down your magic wand list – everything you think of, no matter how madcap it may seem.

_____

_____

_____

_____

2. Next map out the approximate price points you would have as part of your Elegant Business Model. For example, an Internet marketing colleague's prices are:

   - Free
   - $27

- $47 per month
- $1,497
- $2,997
- $16,000 (plus a percentage of sales)

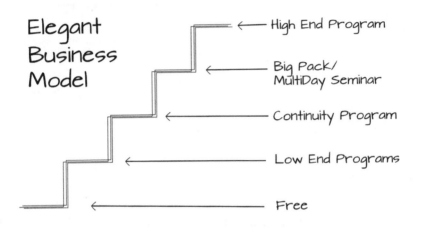

Elegant Business Model

← High End Program

← Big Pack/ MultiDay Seminar

← Continuity Program

← Low End Programs

← Free

Your price points will be dependent on your niche and your brand.

_____

_____

_____

_____

3. Review your magic wand list with your price points in mind.
4. Ask yourself, "Of this list of options, what can I include at each level of product/service?"

Here is an example from the Shift Community for you to model. Before attending our trainings Maura had only one product to sell: her time. Review her complete Elegant Business Model now.

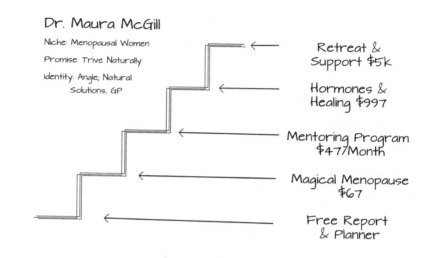

Dr. Maura McGill

Niche: Menopausal Women
Promise: Trive Naturally
Identity: Angle; Natural Solutions, GP

← Retreat & Support $5k

← Hormones & Healing $997

← Mentoring Program $477/Month

← Magical Menopause $67

← Free Report & Planner

To see how it looks in the real world, have a look at Maura's website: www.drmauramcgill.com.

Some replication of content at every level is okay, but there needs to be something at each level that is only available at that level. The value of the product to the client must be much higher than the amount of money they pay for it. As you create your products, always aim for high-perceived value, low cost of delivery. Remember, it's the value of the information that gives the product its price point, not the cost of creation of the product. A DVD costs $1.75 to make even in low quantities using someone like Kunaki.com (check these guys out – you'll be in love!), but the value of that information could be thousands of dollars.

While we're on the subject of production costs, information products are great because they have a high profit margin with little overhead. You can make a product with no money down. Here's an example…

You can host a teleseminar for free using one of many online services, such as FreeConferenceCall.com. Invite your community, record the program using the built-in facilities of the online service, and then you download the Mp3. Now that you're the proud owner of that Mp3 you can give it away online, sell it online (people can pay to download it) or you can turn it into a CD. You can also use sites like Elance.com or vWorker.com to edit your Mp3 into separate, short audios to be released as a mini-course. You can have the audio transcribed and turn it into an article or free report. Whatever format you choose, once the product is made, you can use it over and over without ever having to do that teleseminar again. Cool huh?

On your teleseminar, you can lead it, interview someone or be interviewed by someone you admire who is also appropriate for your community. Newbies, I hope you got that!

BLUEPRINT IN ACTION SNAPSHOT

Australian naturopath, Jodi Chapman, is one of our greatest success stories,demonstrating yet again that it doesn't matter what business you're in – adding speaking is the fastest way to grow your income. And what's more, she didn't even have to get up on stage to do it!

Jodi ran webinars for three months, and each month on average she made $5,000 on the webinars. Not only that, but it also increased her leads and added another $5,000 directly from people coming into the clinic. So speakingincreased her business by $10,000 a month, and she feels this is just the tip of the iceberg!

Jodi is now averaging $40,000-$48,000 per month. On top of that, potential sponsors and supplement companies are now approaching her and people from overseas are contacting her and wanting to work with her. And it's all from working from her passions, and sharing themthrough her Elegant Business Model

See the Elegant Business Model in action at Jodi's website:AdvancedWellness.com.au.

With the Elegant Business Model you can't help but think long term. You create sufficient products that give your clients the opportunity to get started doing business with you for a small amount, knowing that as you fulfill your promise on that product, you can develop trust for further backend products and higher sales down the road.

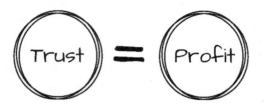

Examples of Information Products and Services:

- Free Reports
- Books
- Ebooks
- Mini Courses
- Teleseminars
- Webinars

- CDs
- DVDs
- Video Courses
- Membership Sites
- Home Study Programs
- Profiling Tools
- Workshops
- Seminars
- Events
- Individual Coaching
- Group Coaching Programs
- Mentoring Programs
- Business in a Box

ACTION
Your Elegant Business Model

Take some time now to design your dream suite of products based on the Elegant Business Model. Have fun!

My Elegant Business Model:

_____

_____

_____

_____

_____

_____

_____

_____

_____

_____

_____

_____

Alert! Don't make any of these products until you've done a few presentations. It's not until you meet your niche in person and deliver your presentation a few times that you will discover what your market really wants more of from you. To get started right away, create only your free gift in return for details.

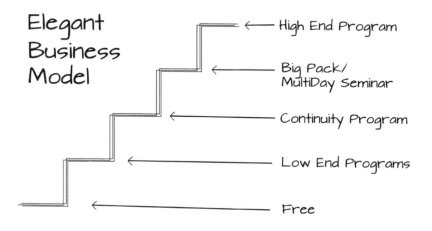

Elegant Business Model

High End Program

Big Pack/ MultiDay Seminar

Continuity Program

Low End Programs

Free

PROFIT PRINCIPLE SIX: PRESENTATION

Have at Least One Solid Effective Presentation that Moves People to Action

How are you doing? Are you still with me? Good, because we're about to put everything from the last five principles into play. So far you've had to wear many hats – innovator, business owner, marketer – but now we're back to what I hope is your favorite – speaker. This is the principle where we take our passion, give it words and make a whole lot of money. We're turning words into wealth.

Before we get into the nuts and bolts of an Effective Presentation, there is one significant point that needs to be addressed. Recognize that as a speaker, you can only really change someone's life if and when they take the next step with you. What do I mean by that? Let's take a look at the average spectrum of presentation outcomes.

First, you have the educational or entertaining speaker whose main outcome is to receive applause. Next, there is the inspirational speaker, who goes beyond applause and whose outcome is to change people's minds. A little further along the spectrum is the transformational speaker, whose outcome is to change people's action. There's room for all of them within the speaking industry, depending on the context for the presentation, but I believe in being a transformational speaker who changes action. You see, here's what the audience is thinking at the end of each of these presentations. With the applause, they're thinking, "You're great." When you've changed their minds, they're thinking, "I'm great." When you've changed their actions, they're thinking, "What's next?" I want you to focus on being a transformational speaker. You can still have your applause, but remember you're there for your audience, not your ego.

PRESENTATION SPECTRUM

Please get it clear in your mind that if you intend to make a real difference in the world, you need to become a great salesperson. I believe transformational leaders like Martin Luther King, Jr., Mother Teresa, Gandhi and Nelson Mandela were/are all amazing salespeople. For me, selling is about creating an environment of influence where people are inspired to take action in accordance with their vision. And that is the essence of an Effective Presentation.

An Effective Presentation is not just a presentation that closes a sale; it's a presentation that changes action. I invite you to start thinking about yourself as a transformational leader. I know you have a message that is close to your heart. You have your passion and your promise, right? Use an Effective Presentation as an opportunity to inspire your audience to take action with *you* to improve their lives. If I know someone wants or needs to learn what I share, it's my duty to inspire them enough to take action with me, because otherwise they may go out and learn it from someone else who a) does not achieve the results that I do or b) is not as ethical I am. Does that open a new way of thinking about sales for you?

BLUEPRINT IN ACTION SNAPSHOT

Thinking about selling my own business from the stage was something I found difficult and sometimes 'improper'. At least that was my belief.[However], during Jo's training and [thanks to]the material she offers on her website, I realized I was doing my audience a disservice, and to me as well.

Jo has changed this belief, and now I understand I should structure my speech so I can sell efficiently in total congruence and integrity. Jo is a marvelous speaker and her storytelling skills coupled with actor's background is pure delight.

I really recommend Jo's approach to public speaking in all that she proposes (workshops, seminars, webinars and newsletters).You will get incredible value and Jo is warm and authentic. I've become addicted to her material...

Michel Delran
IT Architect and Speaker
www.mdelran.mdnovation.com

So what actions could you invite at the end of your presentation?

You're going to learn my seven-step system for inviting action into anything, but here are a few ideas so you can start with the end in mind.

1. Ask your audience to change their behavior.
2. Ask them to donate to a charity.
3. Ask them to join your community.
4. Ask them to book a one-to-one consultation with you.
5. Ask them buy your product or service on the spot.

There is an order and sequence to delivering your presentation, which is covered in the seven steps, but designing it requires looking at it from a different angle. We're going to craft your whole presentation around the final act, which is what you are selling.

The Seven Shifts of a *Profitable* and Effective Presentation

There are Seven Shifts in a Profitable and Effective Presentation. I call them shifts, rather than steps, because your outcome at the end of each session should be to have elicited an emotional *shift* in your audience – not just to have *completed a step*. These seven shifts are spelled out here, assuming you will make a sale at the end of your presentation, but they also work even if you're not closing a sale.

The 7-Shift Effective Presentation Formula ™

1. **Create Connection:** Become a welcome guest and inspire trust and responsiveness in your audience.
2. **Get Permission to Do Your Thing:** Demonstrate credibility and earn the right to be speaking to your audience by illustrating your past results as powerfully as possible.
3. **Engage with Your Content:** Decide on the action you want the audience to take, and craft the backbone of your presentation with this end in mind.
4. **Establish a Need:** Create dissatisfaction in your audience by illustrating where they are vs. where they want to be.
5. **Reveal the Product and Build Tension:** Give a benefit driven description of your product and build up the value.
6. **Make a No-Brainer Offer:** Package up your product with bonuses and ensure you create urgency and take away risk.
7. **Invite Immediate Action:** Finish powerfully with a commanding invitation to buy.

NickCownie @joannamartin **You'll love this – had my first $10,000 hour yesterday using your 7 steps to sell in my presentation. Two words: It... Works!**

www.SuccessDynamicsInstitute.com

Shift One: Create Connection

If you are serious about inspiring people to buy your product, you have to realize that you are not actually selling your product. *You are selling yourself.*

In fact, you should be thinking about the impression you're making to your audience before you ever step on the stage. Let's look at me for a moment. I have to be me writing this book. I have to be me on my website. I have to be me in the emails that come to you once you register for an event. I have to be me from the moment you see me or read about me. One of the most challenging things to do in the whole wide world is to be *you* all of the time. But it's the most important. You have to be authentic. Then from the moment you step on the stage your goal should be to create connection or rapport with your audience in person.

Your goal is to establish two key elements in terms of connection:

1. **Trust:** Your audience should feel like they know you and can count on you.
2. **Responsiveness:** From the beginning you need to be creating an environment and an emotional state in the audience, whereby they respond to each suggestion that you give. (If you ask for hands up, they go up. If you ask them to stand, they stand.) Then when you ask them to buy they are more likely to buy.

Therefore, the first 30 seconds you spend on stage are crucial. You have to remember that the first thing you say – your opening – is like your headline. It must capture your crowd. It's during this time that you must engage the whole room. If you lose them at the beginning you will rarely recapture their attention later. Think about what it's been like for you as an audience member, where within a couple of minutes, you're either invested in a speaker or you're thinking it's a good time to go to the loo!

There are a number of ways to capture your crowd during your opening:

- **Ask enrolling questions**: I like to open by asking questions that I know 100% of the audience will answer with a "Yes." For instance, if I was speaking to an audience of small business owners, I may ask, "By a show of hands, who would like to increase their sales? Who would like to decrease their business headaches?" Everyone who owns a small business would answer yes to at least one of those questions!

- **Engage them in an activity**: Once I ask my questions, I will then follow this up by engaging the crowd in some activity, such as turning to the person next to them and saying, "You're in the right place," or getting them up to meet three people they haven't met yet. By doing this you take the pressure off of yourself to have to rev them up. What's more, they usually have a bit of a laugh during the process, which puts them in a nice receptive state for your message.

- **Tell a GOOD joke**: Please only tell jokes if you're funny! I'm funny in the sense that I'm playful and have fun so that people laugh, but I don't tell canned jokes. I can't pull them off. My dad on the other hand is one of the best joke-tellers that I know. So if humor comes naturally to you, it can be very effective in capturing the crowd. It takes confidence and great timing. It can also go terribly wrong. Have you ever been in front of a speaker who isn't as funny as he thinks he is? Very awkward for everyone involved.

- **Blow them away with facts and stats**: I've seen people start presentations using undeniable facts and statistics, followed by a benefit-focused outline of their talk. For example, here's one my dad uses, "Did you know that 3% of the Australian population suffer from a condition known as hyperhidrosis? You might know it as excessive sweating. Most people believe that if they have this condition they're destined for a life of embarrassment and low self esteem. My name is Peter Martin and in the last three years I have helped hundreds of people to conquer this condition, and tonight I will reveal a way that you can quickly and easily overcome it and live a life of confidence and freedom."

Of course you can use one of these techniques or a mix of them all. Exactly how you open will be a personal style choice, but ensure you do something to capture everyone in the crowd.

Alert! If you do not capture an audience member's attention in the first 30 seconds, you may capture them later, but you have to work SUPER HARD to engage them. Go after 100% involvement.

Shift Two: Get Permission to Do Your Thing

When you start presenting to an audience, it's always best to assume your crowd has no idea who you are, unless you're 100% certain that everyone there has experienced you and your business before. That said, you must get permission from your audience to speak to them and ultimately to sell to them, too.

There are four keys to this step:

1. Explain your style.
2. Confirm your position as the expert.
3. Get buy-in for what you're going to teach them.
4. Get permission for the sale upfront.

1. Explain your style

Early on you want to get permission for, or at least explain, your style. This means if you have anything unusual that people will focus on (such as an accent or interesting looks), explain them first so they're not distracted through the whole presentation.

This is also useful from the point of view of getting the audience to accept your speaking style.

- If it's your first time, tell them. They'll love you for your courage.
- If you want audience interaction, tell them. They'll know what to expect.
- If you're going to go fast to get though content, tell them so they know they'll never be able to keep up with the notes.

I always make a point of telling my audience we'll be having fun while we learn, as I tend to be a bit crazy on stage from time to time! One of my students, an accountant, is quite the opposite. When he first started speaking, he was really boring. So what he started doing was saying, "I'm an accountant. I'm boring. However, I really like how excited you guys get when you save tens of thousands of dollars on your taxes. Is it okay if I share some strategies that will save you tens of thousands of dollars?" Everyone in the room would agree, so he'd continue, "Do I have your permission to be boring while I do it?" And of course, they all said, "Yes." On a side note, by asking permission to be boring, he actually found his footing and grew to be a very successful speaker. He now appears on Sky Business News!

It doesn't matter what style you use in your presentation, as long as you outline it up front, tell your audience why you are that way and then get on with it. You can just be you, as long as you get permission to be you before you start!

2. Confirm your position as the expert

The key here is your credibility statement. Why on earth should these people bother to listen to you? Once you have an answer, you just need to reveal this information to them in a powerful way.

Things to think about as you create a credibility statement:

- What's your story or hook?
- What specific results have you achieved that prove your credibility?
- Do you have any testimonials that prove your credibility?
- Have you written a book?

Now, let me make something clear. Better than a credibility 'statement' is a credibility 'story'. If you've seen me speak live, you probably know that I immediately go into the story about my background. I share the whole story and not just the impressive parts. It's interesting, and people get really engaged!

You don't want to be the speaker who says, "I've made this much money. Here is my house. Here is my car. Don't you want to be me?" Yuck. That will put a bad taste in anyone's mouth. Instead, you want to be elegant about your background, share your story and prove you've earned the right to be on that stage. The results you've achieved are why your audience came to hear you speak, the story is why they *stay* to listen to you.

Alert! If you do not establish credibility, members of your audience will spend your entire presentation trying to prove you wrong or pick out flaws in what you do. So make sure you wow them with your credibility story upfront.

3. Get buy-in for what you are going to teach

It makes sense to give your audience an overview of the formula you're going to teach. Your aim with this step is to have them be desperate to know what you know. You want them to agree that they need to know what you're about to share.

I always check in with my audience right away to confirm they're where they want to be by saying something like, "I went from zero to a quarter of a million dollars in three months. Is that what you came here to learn?" It's like when you're seated on an airplane and the flight attendant reviews the flight number, destination and in-flight service information. That way you can sit back, relax and enjoy the journey.

4. Ask permission for the sale

Permission is vital to the success of your sale. Think about it. If a friend asks you if they can talk to you about something, what do you usually say and do? Most of us (at least the polite ones) say, "Sure," and then sit down with the friend and give them our undivided attention. The same goes with your presentation. If you ask permission, your audience will unconsciously respond like a friend and sit up and take notice. What's more, they will respect how polite you are, which will endear you to them.

Alert! This does not mean it's acceptable to say, "Is it okay if I tell you why I'm so great and then sell you a $3,000 product?" It needs a little finesse!

If I know that at the end of my presentation I will be making an offer on one of my products, I also like to covertly get permission for the sales pitch up front. I have done this many ways, but here's one approach as an example.

After my credibility story I may say, "Is it okay if over the next 90 minutes I tell you exactly how I created these sorts of results and give you the opportunity to do the same in your own business?"

Notice that I don't say, "...how I created these sorts of results and then make you an offer you can't refuse?" I prefer to get permission to "give them an opportunity" or to "take a powerful action", knowing that usually the best action most people could take if they are interested in what I'm teaching is to invest in whatever product I'm offering.

BLUEPRINT IN ACTION SNAPSHOT

*I wanted to give you an update on the incredible explosion I've had in sales since attending Presentation Profits Intensive: My income has gone up by **over £4,000 per month constantly** and I have speaking engagements at least **twice a month.***

Not yet Joey's figures, but boy am I having fun!

I've won a toast masters speech and an election as Vice-Chairman of Nigerians in the Diaspora, and all I did was fine tune my speeches with some "Joey".

Sam Onigbanjo
Business Funding Consultant
London, UK
www.samonigbanjo.com

Shift Three: Engage with Your Content

Your core content, the backbone of your presentation, should reflect your passion for your topic and deliver value on your promise. There is no such thing as too much content, only a too complicated delivery. When you are designing the backbone of your presentation, there are some key things to remember.

1. Know your audience

Think about this for a moment: If you were an accountant speaking to a group of solo-preneurs with limited accounting knowledge, would you present Advanced Tax Planning Strategies for Medium Size Businesses? I sure hope not. Ask yourself the following questions and deliver what your audience wants.

- Who are your audience?
- What level of experience do they have?
- What are their needs, wants, fears and frustrations?
- What are they desperate to know?
- What's their biggest problem?
- What's their greatest dream?

2. Create the content so it sells your product

I know it seems obvious, but I have seen people deliver a presentation with great information and then try and sell a totally unrelated product. For example, if you're a chiropractor and you're doing an evening seminar for a group of prospects where you plan to sell your *12 Weeks to Incredible Back Health* program, I wouldn't recommend doing a presentation on the application of chiropractic in pregnancy.

Before I write any sales presentation, I use my Pre-Presentation Audience Analysis Worksheet to outline effectively what I need to communicate to my audience about the presentation. I designed this tool to help guide me in the right direction before preparing any presentation. All my students also regularly use my 14-question worksheet to prepare effectively for their presentations. Without it, they run the risk of teaching and selling what THEY WANT, not what their audience will PAY MONEY FOR!

I know you want to increase your income through speaking right!? So, to reward you for reading this far, I'm going to give it to you for free! You will find it in the Bonus Resources section of the website.

One of my students, a seven-figure speaker in her own right, was so blown away by this tool. She told me at the training she attended, "This will conservatively add hundreds of thousands of dollars to my income, Jo – thanks!"

BONUS: For your FREE copy of my Pre-Presentation Audience Analysis Worksheet, which will help you to make the most of every speaking opportunity you have, go to: www.presentationprofitsblueprint.com/bonusresources.

3. Work out your timing

Okay, so our next step is to think about how much you should be teaching. And the key determinants are:

a) How much time do you have?
b) How many presentation units do you need?

Don't panic! I know you've never heard the term 'presentation unit' before, and that's because I made it up. I'm cheeky like that. According to the Shift Speaker Training, a presentation unit is defined as the amount of speaking that you can do from one break to the next break.

So if you're speaking at a multi-speaker event and you have one and a half hours from the morning tea break to lunchtime, that's one presentation unit. If you're running a full day event and you have up until morning tea break, then lunch break, then afternoon tea break and then the close, that's four presentation units. Simple enough?

Morning Tea Break   Lunch Break   Afternoon Tea Break   Close

How you structure your content is going to be different depending on how many presentation units you have, but let's take a look at a typical guest speaker, one-presentation-unit presentation (that's about a 60 – 90 minute session).

- Your opening will take 5 – 10 minutes to establish the responsiveness and trust you need.
- Your offer will likely take 10 – 15 minutes to make at the end.
- You should spend no more than eight minutes per point (it has been shown that people's attention span switches off after this time). For each point you share, go through:

* Why the element is important
* A story from your personal experience that illustrates its importance
* One or two strategies your audience can use to apply to their own lives immediately
* A testimonial that proves what you say is true.

- I advise that you stick to three or four key teaching points in total for a 60 – 90 minute presentation. More than that is too overwhelming. Keep in mind that this content will end up being between 50 – 75% of your presentation.

In my one-presentation-unit presentation that I use to sell my Big Pack (my $3,000 Presentation Profits Intensive Workshop or Home Study Program), I teach the Three Steps to Influence. Here's a skeleton of the main teaching content so you can see how this looks in the real world:

ONE-PRESENTATION-UNIT PRESENTATION SAMPLE TEACHING OUTLINE: SHIFT SPEAKER TRAINING'S THREE STEPS TO INFLUENCE

- The definition of influence: It's not pushing, chasing, manipulating, motivating or coercing. The root of the word influence comes from the Latin meaning: "a streaming ethereal power from the stars acting upon the character and destiny of men". (etymonline.com)

- A speaker's financial success is determined by their ability to monetize influence. To the extent that you become a master at the three steps of influence your speaking business will blossom, both financially and in the impact your message has in the world.

- What are the three steps to influence?

  1. **Involve** your audience, by being your true authentic self and meeting them where they are.
  2. **Inspire** your audience by painting out a vision for a new future that resonates with their deepest dreams for themselves. Always walk your talk. Teach great content.
  3. **Invite** your audience to take the next step with you. If one and two are solid, this is a natural next step.

See how concise that is? People walk out knowing that if they want to influence from the stage, there are three tools they can implement right away.

Of course, you may have hundreds of tools and strategies surrounding your topic, but you want to pick just a few to introduce to your audience and then let them know where they can get the rest if they choose. For example, if you've written a book called *101 Tips to Uncovering Hidden Profits in Your Business*, an ideal presentation model would be:

- Tip 17 – Contact your clients.
- Tip 32 – Create an information product.
- Tip 78 – Ask for referrals.

By numbering the tips, your audience realizes that these are just three of at least 78 things you could teach them. Do you think they'll be interested in finding out the others? Of course they will. If you use this model, don't be afraid to give away your best bits. Remember, the funniest parts of the movie are always used in the trailer to get you into the cinema!

4. Choose your approach

When it comes to the proper approach for the backbone of your presentation, there have always been two schools of thought.

Some speakers will load on the content and high value information, lavishing their audience with all the details of what they need to do and *how* to do it. These types of speakers operate with the belief that their audience will respond, "Wow! If they give me this much information for free, imagine what great quality their product or service will be if I buy it."

Other speakers may *seem* to say an awful lot, but actually don't teach very much. They are often quite fast paced and entertaining in their delivery. They may tell you a lot of *what* to do, but very little, if any, *how-to* information. Their assumption is that by not giving content, their audience will have to buy the product to get the assistance they really need.

Both schools of thought are right and both work. And generally any mix between education and entertainment is fine. But remember, you want to be a transformational speaker, so keep that in mind as you choose your approach and make a decision that feels comfortable for you.

Personally, I opt for lots of great content, with enough entertainment factor that people get out of their heads and into their hearts. But you can find your way!

Shift Four: Establish Need

The next phase of your presentation should establish a need for change in your audience. As you get more proficient, you can make this phase happen concurrently during the backbone of your presentation, but to begin with you can think about it as a separate section if it makes it easier.

Your main goal in this part of the presentation is to create tension between where they are and where they want to be. Once again, there are two tried and true ways to make this work.

1. Pain Motivated

Using this strategy you identify your audience's pain, aggravate it, rub some salt in the wound and then demonstrate how your product will take their pain away. This is moving them from pain to no problems.

2. Inspiration Motivated

Using this strategy you paint a bright, inspiring vision of the future and point out all of the wonderful things that can be possible for them in this new future. You then demonstrate how far from this ideal they are currently. This is moving them from no problems to inspiration.

I used to believe the only way to get people motivated was to get them feeling their pain and solve their problem for them. However, recently I saw one of the most graceful sales processes, selling over $240,000 over 60 minutes to a small group, that was *entirely* inspiration motivated.

The thing to realize, though, is this: When you're starting out it's easier to get people associated to their pain, than to their visions of the future. So in the beginning, pain motivation is easiest to practice.

Ultimately, whichever path you choose is totally up to you, but here are a few more questions to help you decide.

1. What is your product?
   a. Does it help people to overcome a pain (in business, life, relationships, health)?
   b. What pain(s) specifically?
2. How will they feel once the pain has gone?
3. Does it help people who are comfortable create an even better life?
   a. How will they feel when they use your product?
   b. What will they get that they are currently missing out on?

Once you have answered these questions, you will have the basic points for establishing a need for your product. It's then simply a case of delivering it in a powerful and compelling way.

Establishing need is creating tension between where they are now and where they could be in the future with your product or service.

BLUEPRINT IN ACTION SNAPSHOT

I have had the opportunity to work with several speaker trainers. Lots of them had interesting things to say, but none of them helped me create the kinds of results in my business that Joanna Martin did.

In the first presentation I did after my training with Jo, I closed $80,000 in new business from the stage in two hours and got 14 new clients, and it was easier than ever before!

The techniques she taught me have created immeasurable results and it was the best investment I have ever made in my business.

Kelly O'Neil
Award Winning Marketing Strategist,
Author and Speaker
Los Angeles, CA

Step Five: Reveal the Product and Further Build Tension

Before your presentation you should think long and hard about your product and how you will package it to create an offer that is so compelling for your audience that it becomes a no-brainer.

Think about these things when designing your offer:

- Who is your audience and what is it they want from you?
- What price point is reasonable based on what you know of your audience?
- What is the central product: CD, DVD, book, consumer product, seminar, consulting, etc.?
- What bonuses could you add to build the value to an extreme level? Always be thinking about bonuses that are high-perceived value to the customer, but low cost for you to deliver. I endeavor to come up with enough good quality bonuses that the value of the bonuses exceeds the value of the actual product.
- Could you make a two-tiered product offering, perhaps a basic version of your pack and a deluxe version with an extra special bonus or two? Now your audience won't be thinking, "Do I buy or not?" They will be thinking, "Which package do I buy?"

Let's break it down in a little more detail. The first step in creating your own irresistible offer is to get clear on the packaging of your product – how you bundle the products together. The reason is that I believe you have to work almost as hard to sell a $27 product from stage as selling a $27,000 product. So it's best to pre-determine the spending capacity of your audience and the amount of time you have to sell, and then bundle up a package especially for them.

1. Selling **Products** from the Stage

Products may include consumer goods, computers, clothing, cosmetics, home wares and business resources such as information products and seminars.

Always look at how you can package together a few products to make a pack, rather than just selling one DVD or one lipstick. If you sell beauty products, you could try the Ultimate Spring Beauty Package complete with foundation, lipstick, mascara and scent, rather than trying to do individual sales. Or if you have books, CDs and DVDs available for sale, bundle them up together and create a Big Pack (like my Presentation Profits Home Study Program) that provides a complete resource for your clients.

2. Selling **Services** from Stage

Services may include massage, chiropractic, naturopathy, accounting, personal training, financial planning, legal services, consulting, coaching, music lessons, laser hair removal, etc.

If you're selling any of these services from stage, it's a good idea to bundle up sessions and offer a reduced rate. For example, rather than selling one massage, instead do a '10 sessions for the price of seven' bundle. If you are concerned that offering a discount on your services will mean there's not enough profit for you, it sounds like your margins are already too skinny. If that's the case, the first thing to do is raise your prices. My personal trainer put her price up from $70 to $85 an hour and she didn't lose a single client because we all love her so much. That said, my marketing coach once told me that you can afford to put your prices up by 10% and lose 30% of your clients and still be ahead. So make sure you are priced at a point where even your discounted rate feels good for you.

3. Give Your Package a Sexy Name

Here are four examples:

- Fast Forward Business Coaching Package (Seven, two-hour sessions over three months)
- Protect Your Ass–ets Legal Package (10 hours of asset protection consulting and services)
- New Sexy You Personal Training Package (20 sessions over three months)
- Million Dollar Makeover Coaching Package (12 months of coaching to add $100,000 to the bottom line)

4. Give Your Audience Options

When deciding on how you package your products, it's a good idea to give options, but...

Do not give an A or B option.
Instead, use an A or A + B option.

Say in your suite of products you have a six-DVD set and coaching package that you offer.

Rather than offer your audience:

A six-DVD set: Tips to Maximize Business Profit for $997

OR

Six sessions of one-on-one business coaching for $1,497

Instead offer them:

Basic Pack – Six-DVD set: Tips to Maximize
Business Profit for $997

OR

Deluxe Pack – Six-DVD set: Tips to Maximize Business
Profit **PLUS** six sessions of one-on-one business
coaching for $1,497.

Do you see the difference? So will your profits.

BLUEPRINT IN ACTION SNAPSHOT

*We sold a 12-week webinar course: "The PT Dream
Lifestyle Transformation Program", premier and
basic. I did the exact same close that Jo did, with the
premier package coming in at $1,497 on the day (down
from value of $9,413!). There were 20 people in the
room and 12 signed! We signed up eight people on
premier and four basics!*

*I had to go and stand in the corner after I finished
the close because I couldn't stop the silly grin spread-
ing over my face as people literally ran to the back of
the room to be in our special top four!*

Kat Eden
Personal Trainer and Health / Performance Coach
Melbourne, Victoria
www.bodyincredible.com
www.womanincredible.com

Continue To Build Tension When Revealing the Product

By this stage in your presentation your audience should be feeling a little uncomfortable, and that's good. They will be aware of the fact that they're not getting the results they deserve. You've created an emotional need for them and now it's time to clearly and confidently reveal your product. The biggest problem some speakers have is in their close. They deliver this elegant presentation and then when they get to the close they become some sort of freak. I urge you to relax and be the same way during the close that you were throughout the rest of the presentation. Do you think you can do that?

Imagine you have a rubber band. From this point until you solve their problem by making your compelling offer on your product, your job is to stretch that band further and further and increase the tension more and more in your audience. The tension is the difference between where they see themselves now and where they would like to be at some point in the future.

This segment is the substance of the close. During this segment you can introduce:

- Why you created your product (briefly, what problem does it solve?)
- What your product is called
- Who it's for
- Who it's not for (takeaway selling)
- A benefit-focused description of what it does and what it includes
- Proof of what you say is true with further testimonials if needed.

The three fundamental desires that most members of most audiences will share are:

1. Desire for more time
2. Desire for more money
3. Desire for more quality relationships (family).

If you're able to show congruently how your product will give your prospect more time, more money and more quality with their family, you're halfway toward closing the sale. It's what we all want at some level – the magic pill that gives us more time and money to do what we want, with whom we want.

This also covers the two main objections that most people have to any sale:

1. I don't have the time.
2. I don't have the money.

So if you can demonstrate to your audience that your product gives them more time and more money, you've not only overcome two main objections to the sale, but you've fulfilled two fundamental desires in one easy step.

I can almost hear the objections from you now: "But I sell naturopathic services. That doesn't give you more money," or, "I'm presenting and selling relationship counseling. That doesn't give you more time." Trust me, you can make anything give you more time and money if you try hard enough.

Example One: Naturopathic Services

"This will increase your health and vitality and you will find you operate with a much clearer mind. You'll get more done, more effectively, giving you more time to spend doing the things you want, like spending time with your family. What's more, our services will save you thousands in medical bills. Undertaking a course of care with our therapists is like us writing you a check for all of the thousands of dollars you will save with doctors, dentists and specialists. This won't cost you money; it will save, even make you money!"

Example Two: Relationship Counseling

"How much time are you spending per day stressing about your marriage? How much time do you spend walking on eggshells around each other? When you break through this with our counselors and reconnect in a meaningful way, it will be like you've just received a gift of an extra two, three or four hours per day to spend with your loved ones, your family and your children. What's more, this can make you money. What a bold statement, huh? But we've had countless couples who, within weeks of working with us, find themselves performing more effectively at work, getting more done. In fact, Jane Smith attributes her promotion and an extra $5,600 a year directly to her counseling with her husband, Peter, and their counselor, Sally."

You get the idea, right? Of course, it has to be true. And if you can back up each bold claim with a success story, like in this last example, even better.

BLUEPRINT IN ACTION SNAPSHOT

I was really struggling to get along to your three-day event. I really had to scrounge and scrape. But from there things have changed a lot in the last 10 months.

One of the best moves I made was to set myself up to do my own event the week after your training. I'd never spoken on stage. I'd done some back-of-room work for others, but this was my first time at my own seminar. It was definitely the first time I'd tried to close.

At the first one we had 18 people and a couple of them joined our continuity program. That was okay.

But I do exactly what you tell me to do – I take the Formula every time. I go through my notes every time. So I tweaked some stuff after that first presentation. At the second one we closed 80% of the room. I did my close just as you said, and as I was walking down the aisle I literally had people handing me order forms! It was so cool! I get chills just thinking about it!

But one of the things that is so great about the Shift programs is the level of people you meet at the events. The people I have met at your event have been such a support for me over the last 10 months.

I'd say we're at the $300,000 to $350,000 mark since starting 10 months ago. I couldn't have done it without you Joey.

Leela Cosgrove
Information Marketer and Speaker
Melbourne, Victoria
www.leelacosgrove.com

Don't Rush as You Reveal Your Product

The reason I am relaxed, clear and confident during my close is because, as I said way back at the beginning of the book, I am committed to giving my audience enough information for them to make a decision on whether they want to continue their journey with me. I'm unattached to what decision they make. My audience has given me a whole hour or even a whole day of their time. I'm going to honor them by giving them enough information to make a decision now (because I want them to take immediate action, right?).

Here's the thing. When your audience is in your room, it's not about them being connected to you as the speaker. It's not about all of the good things you do. If you're a good speaker, when someone is sitting in your room they get connected to their source. They get connected to their motivations in life. They get connected to what's possible for them. You being connected to *your* source as the speaker allows them to be connected to *their* source. That's the power of speaking. That's the power of being a transformational leader.

When each member of your audience walks out of the room, what do they meet? Life. Yes, if you're someone who attends seminars fairly often, you understand the sense of camaraderie that is there. Everyone is so excited, sharing ideas and making plans. But when people get home, the environment is just as they left it and there are usually a few wet blankets. And get this, Greg and I are both very abundant in thinking and both are very inspired by our business, but if we're not in an event together, I'm his wet blanket. He's my wet blanket. You have to get home and raise that person to the same level of possibility as you, which can be no small feat.

You want your audience members to be committed to the next step and make the decision with you so they get what they want and need. And for them to do that, you have to give them all of the information they need to make that decision. And you need to deliver it slow enough that they actually get it. There's no need to rush!

Features and Benefits

As you are revealing your product, walk your audience through your product and highlight each feature and benefit. What's the difference? Well, a feature is what the product is. A benefit is how it will change their life.

FEATURE	BENEFIT
Characteristic of your product	Result of Applying the Feature
Answers the question: What does it include?	Answers the question: What's in it for me?
Examples:	Examples:
• Six DVDs on presentation skills • Two hours of personal time with me • 80 GB hard disk drive and 1GB memory	• Powers of persuasion to get what you want every time • A residual $10,000/month with no further effort from you • Fast startup to give you more time to enjoy with your family

A feature describes your product. A benefit sells your product because it shows the prospect how it will change their life. Which do you think is better to use in your presentations? The answer is both. Never give a feature without following it up with a benefit. Otherwise, you'll spark the question "So what?" from your audience. And that means fewer sales.

Now that we're clearer on the differences between a feature and a benefit, it's time to get more intimate with your product and describe it in terms of the benefits it provides to your customer. You may find it easier to start with a list of the features. Most business owners know their product intimately, so this is naturally where you will feel most comfortable.

Once you have a list of features, add a benefit to each of them. A good strategy is to imagine you are your ideal customer and to look at each feature and ask yourself, "What does that mean for me?"

Let's say the product you're selling is a one-day sales training for small business owners. Start by listing out all of the features of the product in the first column and then the benefits in the next. When you start to deliver your presentation, you will always link your feature to a benefit.

Try it out here:

"In this sales training you will learn how to create rapport with anyone *which means* that you will be able to connect with and persuade people who ordinarily wouldn't give you the time of day..."

"You'll learn the Powerful Six Step Sales Process *so that* you can reliably and routinely produce the same results with a replicable system *which means* you can predict your cash flow month to month and there are no surprises."

Even though you have a complete list of features and benefits, both general and specific, the truth of the matter is that people buy from you for a very small number of reasons. I like to call these reasons your customer's Pareto Motives. This is my shorthand for the top 20% of reasons why people buy.

You have no doubt heard of Pareto's Principle: 20% of your activity gets you 80% of your results, 20% of your customers give you 80% of your business (and 20% of them give you 80% of your headaches!), 20% of your carpet gets 80% of the wear, and so on and so forth. It's the same in sales: **20% of your benefits close 80% of your sales**.

So as you reveal your product, it should look like this:

20% of time on features / 80% of time on benefits
Of the time you're speaking about benefits, 80% of your time should be spent on the 20% of benefits you know most people want!

Fourteen DVDs is a feature. Sitting at home, going at your own pace, implementing as you go along and putting systems in place that will generate over a million dollars a year – those are benefits.

BLUEPRINT IN ACTION SNAPSHOT

This process is phenomenal and we have constantly made money to prove it!

Joanna goes through the whole process of how to sell on stage and what she explained was just phenomenal; I'd never seen anything like it. So, what this enabled us to do was change our two-day workshop that we were running to a three-day workshop. And now we've never looked back!

We did everything she told us to do. Since that workshop we've done millions of dollars in sales. If you want to learn how to sell from the stage, you have to listen to Joanna. She knows her stuff, and she will change your results, guaranteed. Go for it!

Matt Clarkson
eBay speaker and Entrepreneur
Gold Coast, Australia
www.biddingbuzz.com

Shift Six: Make a No-Brainer Offer

Your audience should be almost agitated and wanting to jump out of their seat. Your next job is to give them a reason to buy *now*. Here are a few ways to shape a no-brainer offer:

1. Bonuses plus Discount

The easiest way to shape an offer is to add great bonuses to the package and discount it. But your bonuses must have real value. The bonuses I put into my offers have all been paid for as stand-alone products, prior to me adding them. You want your bonuses to have inherent value.

2. Scarcity

If something is perceived as scarce, the value goes up. Human nature says that people want what they can't have.

So when designing your offer think about what limiter you can put on it.

A must read book if you are serious about selling is *Influence: The Psychology of Persuasion*, by Robert Cialdini. In it he outlines the rules that govern influence. All of them are vital to the success of any platform seller, but one that works perfectly to create urgency in your crowd is The Law of Scarcity: we all want something that we can't have.

So, your offer must be urgent. Give them a deadline. Explain the deadline. Stand firm on your deadline.

Options for creating urgency are based on limited time, limited number, or both:

- Seminar only specials – only valid while they are at the seminar
- Extra special bonus for the first x number of people to buy
- Limited spaces available at the course
- Charter memberships
- First x number of successful applications.

Please note that I am a great believer that these limiters must always be true!

3. Reason Why

A good reason why is necessary to relieve any doubts about your offer. Some people may think your offer is too good to be true or, if you're discounting it, there must be something wrong with it. So when you do a price drop, always tell them why and always tell the truth. You could try something like, "Because we only have room for nine more clients on our books, I am going to make an offer that will be available for the first nine of you who choose to take action immediately. This is much more elegant than, "There's only nine spots left so hurry now."

4. Guarantee

What guarantee can you make on your product or service that removes all risk for the customer? The bigger and bolder the guarantee, the more you will sell.

Your guarantee can make or break your offer. So in order to develop an excellent guarantee, ask yourself: **What perceived risk does my client face when dealing with me?**

Here is an example of one of my own guarantees:

EXAMPLE OF A BOLD GUARANTEE:

PUT ALL THE RISK ON US – 100% MONEY BACK GUARANTEE

Join my mentoring program today and try it out for a full 30 days. If at the end of that time you're not convinced that it's value for money, for whatever reason, just ask and we'll refund your subscription immediately. AND you get to keep the bonuses (valued at over $450) as our way of saying, "Sorry for wasting your time."

My personal feeling is that if you offer a guarantee, honor it. Too many people in this business offer a guarantee and then when you take them up on it, they fight you about it. If one is requested, give the money back graciously with an open heart and a big smile. In doing so, you are just as likely to create a raving fan. I have had people ask for their money back in the past and then go on to continue to refer clients to me. Just because it's not right for them, doesn't mean it's not right for their friends.

Short and simple, if you're good at what you do, give a guarantee.

> **Alert!** Don't wimp out when delivering your offer. Your delivery must be punchy, confident and clear. Don't apologize!

Shift Seven: Invite Immediate Action

Once you've outlined and inspired people with your offer, you have to tell them exactly what to do. The reason for this is that if you've done a good job with the connection step, they may not want to be rude and break the connection to go and buy what you're offering. Therefore, you must invite them to buy.

Remember the old adage: If you confuse them, you lose them. So make sure at the end of your presentation they know exactly where to go, and what to do to take the next step. Spell it out.

I like to use embedded commands in this step. An embedded command is a three-step command where the first two steps tell you how to do it and the last step tells you what to do.

Think about some common three-step commands you've heard all of your life:

- Ready, aim, fire!
- Lights, camera, action!
- On your mark, get set, go!

Now see how you can use the same technique in your invitation to action:

> **Josh Williams** Awesome! I reckon your training generated close to $50k in my business in 2010 :) I had one trip to Melbourne with a promoter where I had 90 minutes on stage and left with $10k thanks to your advice...
> Friday at 17:44 · Unlike · 👍 2 people
>
> www.myvids.com.au

- I invite you right now to close your notebook, go to the back and **register for this seminar**.
- Take your form, grab your pen, and **fill in this form now**.
- Stop doubting yourself, listen to your gut and **invest in this home study course.**

The embedded command is great. Once you give it, get off the stage. Turn up the music to keep the energy high. You've worked hard to create a sense of urgency and excitement, so here are a few more suggestions to help you achieve the optimum results.

How NOT To Finish Your Presentation

1. Do not open up for questions at the end of your close. What emotional state comes up in the audience when someone asks a question? Doubt. Doubt is not an action taking state.

2. Do not let someone make an announcement at the end of your presentation. If someone announces that the owner of car B45WR has left their lights on, everyone will be thinking, "Whose car is that? Is that my car? Thank goodness that's not my car." And your offer is forgotten.

3. Do not waffle like an idiot. Just finish, close your mouth and get off the stage. Gracefully and elegantly walk to the back table. Leave your microphone on so that as you're answering people's questions, everyone else in the room is hearing the answers.

4. Do not make apologies for the sale after you do it. This will cut your sales in half. An apology sounds nice, but it undoes all of the good work you did. And if people walk out without taking the next step, they leave without the full gift you can give them.

5. Don't ask for testimonials after you close. When you hand someone a microphone you're handing over control of the energy in the room. What could possibly go wrong? They ramble, go long, get off target or incite doubt. Then you have to redirect your audience's attention back to you and your offer. Uncomfortable, right?

Order Forms

An important component to your invitation to action and your sales process in general is your order form. Without getting into too much detail here, you absolutely want to have your order forms printed and at the ready to support whatever package you are offering at an event. As a special gift to you, on the Resources page, I have included my order form checklist and a sample of one of my own order forms. Check them out www.presentationprofitsblueprint.com/ bonusresources.

An Effective Presentation is a skill that everyone can use in their business. It's a system and a structure you can implement into any occupation to increase your sales and bring you closer to the lifestyle of your dreams.

BLUEPRINT IN ACTION SNAPSHOT

I spoke yesterday at a no-sell exhibition and used your 'lead people' strategy to get £1,500 of sales. :-)

This paid for the event and we generated serious coaching and speaking leads for high paying opportunities. I also got booked by a promoter for two events next year at their BIG Industry Event. They were, and I quote, "blown away" by my presentation and how I got so many people to walk over 500 meters to buy!

I have now secured over £30,000 of ADDITIONAL coaching client revenue and Franchise Leads as a result of this presentation – you have to just love this business.

Thanks Jo and team; all strategies I learned at Shift Speaker Training.

Paul Avins
Founder of The Business Wealth Club Franschise
Oxford, UK
www.thebusinesswealthclub.com

ACTION
Outline Your Effective Presentation

Using the structure of the Seven Elements, begin to outline your own presentation. Be as detailed as you can. You may want to do this on a whiteboard or flip chart, in a journal or on your computer. Give yourself plenty of room to write and time to complete.

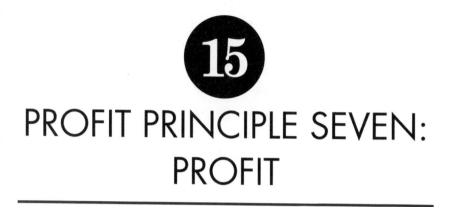

PROFIT PRINCIPLE SEVEN: PROFIT

Leveraging Your Effort and Automating Your Business for Profit

Everything we've done so far – the planning, preparation and implementation of the strategies outlined in this blueprint – culminate here, achieving and maintaining your dream lifestyle. If you've fully participated and have expanded your comfort zone throughout this process, than you may already be making a very decent cash flow. I hope you are experiencing firsthand that speaking and selling from stage is one of the most lucrative business strategies around. Now it's time to systemize and automate as much as possible so you can stop trading time for money and create a sustainable freedom inside of your business.

Alert! As a speaker who closes sales from stage, it is easy to see high figures such as $10,000, $40,000 or even $250,000 from a 90-minute presentation and to think that your business is doing great. But business is a game of **profit** not **revenue**. So you need to focus on maintaining profits and maximizing output from low amounts of effort.

Once you are generating cash flow from speaking, there are a few key areas you will want to optimize to make sure you have the Lifestyle Business you deserve. Through smart choices in the following areas you will discover it is possible to run a multi-million dollar business with a handful of staff and still have plenty of time to do what you like!

Hiring the Right Staff and Making Good Use of Outsourcing

Take a look at any successful speaking business or any business where speaking is a component of the marketing and you will discover a solid team.

Sure, I'm the front woman of our business, but I'm not the only one keeping things moving. Here's a snapshot of what's going on in my business right now at 4:50pm this Friday afternoon in London:

1. I'm happily typing this over a Pimms (it's nearly knock-off time after all) after shooting some video in my home studio 15 minutes ago.
2. Greg is trying to contact the United States to set up a new contract with a company we are using to outsource.
3. Tamara is editing a free video training series, perhaps even one of the ones you've seen on my website.
4. Vanessa, who works in Australia, is hopefully asleep but while we slept last night she created four new web pages, adjusted the functionality of our website, loaded up some blog posts and sent out emails for me.
5. Larisa is surfing the Internet on my behalf and bookmarking our blog with social networking sites.

6. Jo H is sleeping, too, hopefully (also in Australia), but while we slept last night she had accountability calls with all of our Australian Platinum members to make sure they are actually implementing the type of information I'm sharing with you here.
7. Sam is dreaming sweet dreams, but while I slept last night she was working on creating 10 search engine optimized articles for me based on audios I have created.
8. Kylie is preparing our BAS return (a bookkeeping phenomenon that must happen quarterly in Australia). She probably is awake even though she's Australian; she seems to be a night owl.
9. A chap in Romania, whose name I don't actually know because Vanessa manages him, is redesigning another website for me (for one of the other businesses in which I'm a silent partner).
10. A lovely lady in the Philippines is transcribing an audio I recorded the other day.

So while it looks like I'm a busy little bee, I'm not really. Nine extraordinary human beings, who love what they do and are great at it doing it, support me. Only two are full time staff members. The rest are part of our wider team who contract to us and other entrepreneurs to provide great services at very reasonable rates.

Tim Ferriss, author of the book, *The 4-Hour Work Week*, would be proud – although he would've outsourced the writing of the Blueprint, too. Call me old-fashioned, but I still like to hold onto the important things.

With the Internet and international currency exchange being what it is these days, you can pay someone next to nothing for you, which is a small fortune for them, to assist you with something they can do better than you anyway.

Here are some links to the places we find good people. You'll recognize them from earlier in the book:

- vWorker.com
- Elance.com
- oDesk.com

Now, I have a confession to make. I'm dreadful at managing virtual staff, which is why I hired someone who is a technical whizz and is good at managing our international counterparts. I also use a virtual assistant (VA) company, whose owner lives around the corner from me. So she comes over and drinks lots of coffee with me personally and then goes and manages her staff on my behalf. In the United

BLUEPRINT IN ACTION SNAPSHOT

Before working with Joanna, I was trying to do pretty much everything in the business. I was very 'busy' and wasn't getting the results with the 'busy-ness'. But now I am able to organize my time and prioritize my tasks much more effectively. I am more in tune with who I am and what's important to me and am more comfortable delegating tasks, which means my own everyday tasks are much more enjoyable and I am getting better business results from myself and my clients!

Ruth Thirtle
Networking and Business Development Specialist
Australia
BusinessNetworker.co

States, Australia and the United Kingdom, there are individuals like this who can bridge that gap for you.

Managing and Creating Websites that Support Your Speaking

When I woke up on Thursday morning, Greg greeted me with the news that we made $6,027.33 while we were sleeping. Mmmm, nice. I should sleep more often. I would love to claim responsibility for that, but it's in large part due to the websites we have set up that sell our products for us at any time of the day and night.

Succeeding in the speaking business is as much, if not more, about mastering the Internet and copywriting these days as it is about mastering the platform. And if you have no clue about any of this, I highly recommend finding a partner or staff member who does, because it's an essential element for freeing you up from time-for-money on stage.

The key component to leveraging your time and resources is creating at least one subscription program as part of your Elegant Business Model. Did you know it's just as easy to sell something that you get paid for once, as it is to sell something that you get paid for every month?

There are many types of subscription models you could use. Here are a few for your consideration:

1. Text Classes
2. Audios (teleseminars or pre-recorded audios)
3. Webinars
4. Videos
5. Live Events
6. A mixture of any and all of these.

You're limited only by your creativity. But this key piece will give you reliable income every month to cover your bills, staff costs and even make a tidy profit of its own. And when you run your live workshops it's all just ice cream, remember? We talked about this in Principle Five.

Navigating the Minefield of Software and Choosing the Right Back Office Program

The challenge that nearly grounded our speaking business to a halt was software. In this day and age you have to run your business online and it seemed that all of the software had been designed for purely online businesses.

One thing you will discover when you start speaking is that great pieces of online software like auto responders are not great for anything other than a tiny speaking business, because more often than not your clients give you their email address on a form at an event, not online. So what? Well, if you use AWeber.com as your email auto responder, the first message they get comes from a company they've never heard of called AWeber, asking them to confirm their email address. Yes, you can customize the message, but it's still not good when they've paid for products that you can't send to them because they haven't confirmed their email address.

Similarly, if you use PayPal to collect payments and PayPal recognizes someone's credit card number as you enter it from your event form, PayPal helpfully says, "Hi Robert, welcome back. Please enter your password," which is not helpful if you are not Robert and don't know what his password is.

So, speaking businesses, which are a unique mixture of online and offline strategies, require a well-integrated software solution. Greg (or as we call him, Greggle) spent months looking for something to fit the bill, and finally we found something that after a few smart customizations now suits our business perfectly.

You can start small with something like 1ShoppingCart. com. Many speakers run their whole system off of this and make up for its insufficiencies with extra staff hours and offline systems.

To get started running events, check out Eventbrite. com. They are a great service that allows you to get a web-site together in less than 15 minutes to sell tickets to your workshop or seminar.

But eventually you will want something in-house, integrated and all-encompassing. When you're ready for that, check out our SecretWeaponSoftware.com. You'll be dealing with my very own in-house techie who understands how and why we do business the way we do. She was so impressed with the software that she asked us if she could sell it to our clients, and because of the dearth of choices in the market place, we agreed.

Automating and Outsourcing Product Fulfilment

Once you get your Elegant Business Model in place and are selling millions of dollars worth of product per year, you'll want to get it out of the spare bedroom! But even before then you can use fulfillment houses at a reasonable rate to create and ship your CDs, DVDs and manuals.

Let's define a few things up front. You need someone to:

- Duplicate your product
- Package it
- Store it
- Ship it

These are four different tasks, but oftentimes can be done by the same company. Especially in the United States, they will do all of it, handle customer enquiries and even accept returns (though I haven't seen one of those outside of the States).

Things to be aware of when finding someone:

1. Do they create the product in-house? They may outsource their duplication and charge a lot for it if they are just a drop shipper. If they create the product in-house they will usually have minimum print runs (except somewhere like Kunaki.com, which just does CDs and DVDs one at a time).
2. Do they ship small amounts of product at a time or do they have minimum amounts?
3. Do they store product at their facility and do they charge for it?

Basically, do your due diligence and ask for a few quotes and you'll do okay.

Once you're selling quite a bit of product, it will be easy to get good rates for lower volumes. It's just when you're starting out it might be more expensive per unit, but it's better than having a garage full of DVDs you can't sell. If you have a good software system (like the Secret Weapon) it will automatically notify your drop shipping company and you don't need to even think about it!

Setting up a Smart Business Structure to Protect Your Assets

I hope you succeed in the speaking business. I hope you go international. And I hope you have to deal with the challenges of operating in three different currencies in three different countries like we do! Again, a speaking business is a little different to an online business. Online, the currency of the Internet is United States Dollar (USD). But try and sell a Brit or an Aussie something at a seminar on their own home turf in USD and they will turn up their nose at it, even if they really want it.

If you're selling at events, the currency has to be local. Period.

Greg has navigated these challenges for us with aplomb, but the moral of the story is you need to have a great business advisor, not just with regard to currencies, but also with your general business structure. At the very least, make sure you are incorporated. A few other points to note:

- Can my software handle multi-currency?
- Can my merchant facility handle multi-currency?
- Am I fulfilling tax obligations in each country in which I operate?
- Does my accountant understand the international tax law enough to support me in making the best decisions here?
- Are my assets protected should someone sue me?
- Is my IP protected correctly?

Yes, it's overwhelming and you don't have to have all of this figured out right away. But should your speaking career take off (which it will!), my greatest wish is that your daily challenge becomes not, "How do I make ends meet this month?" but, "What's the best way to structure my international affairs so I can get my tax bill to less than a million dollars this year?" Better quality problem!

Caring for Your Customers and Giving Them a WOW Experience

If you already care about people, which I'm sure you do, then you need to have a system in place where you are always striving to make an awesome experience every time you have contact with your customers. It becomes a 'wow' experience and you stand out head and shoulders above your competitors. Your goal of customer service is to leave people you connect with happier than when you found them. A service should provide the customer with more than a product or an action taken on their behalf.

Your customers are not just the people who pay for your goods and services.

Your customers include:

- Clients
- Friends and associates
- Joint venture partners and affiliates
- Vendors and service providers
- All staff

Good customer service doesn't just mean happy customers. It means continued success, increased profits, higher job satisfaction, improved company and organization morale, better teamwork and market expansion of your services and products. Plus, it's downright good karma!

Remember, your customers are part of your community. Your community is your business. From the moment they have first contact with you, they should experience phenomenal customer care – from your presence on the stage, to your sales team and systems at the sales tables, to your representatives on the phone, your email correspondence and your team's response if your customers are dissatisfied or unhappy. Everything matters. Every action is an opportunity to wow your customer. Care for them, keep them happy, and your business will boom.

BLUEPRINT IN ACTION SNAPSHOT

Elaine and I both had suffered with ME, also known as chronic fatigue or fibromyalgia. So, we decided we wanted to make a difference to others who did, too. So we set up a little a basic website and we had people from all over the world contacting us and wanting our help and we were only just going to do something small as a hobby alongside what we were already doing.

However, with the impact that our little basic website had, we realized we needed to do something a lot bigger but had no idea how to do it.

Thanks to your program, we managed to develop a fully holistic recovery program that enables sufferers wherever they are in the world to be able to access a recovery program that's online.

But even then, we weren't making quite the impact we wanted to make. So we took another step…

We've now developed a practitioner training element to what we do, which enables the sufferers coming through our online recovery program to work one-on-one with the practitioners that have been trained by us in our 'Chrysalis Effect Program'. We launched it with a 3-day training for practitioners.

Well, we had 19 attend our January Practitioner Training at £997 a ticket.   So, we had about £15,000 coming within a month, which was amazing.   But still we knew that we couldn't actually give them all they needed in those three days.   So we offered a 12 month master class, and of 19 people, we had 8 people join us so that brought in over £30,000 income for us at one event.   It didn't all come in at once; some of them are paying monthly over 12 months, but the shift that we took from that was incredible.   We were struggling to bring in £1,000 a month with the original program, and now we made £30,000 in a weekend.   We were just so shocked - and we learned that model from you.

It's so exciting because now our clients learn from us and they want to do it to make a difference to people, and really that's why we're doing it.   Yes, making money is great, but we have got a vision to make a difference and that's what drove us to create this business model and now its succeeding!

Kelly Oldershaw and Elaine Wilkins
Pioneers of ME and CFS Recovery
Brighton, UK
www.getyourlifebackfromme.com

PUTTING THE BLUEPRINT INTO ACTION

I would like you to be honest with yourself for a moment and really decide if you want to create a lifestyle of freedom through speaking. Because if you aren't committed, if you don't have the passion, all of the techniques in the world won't matter. Sometimes we wait for the secret to be revealed before we get into action – isn't it true? We think there's some special thing that no one's told us yet. But there isn't. You just need to do what everyone's been telling you to do. It's actually really simple, but it's not easy because you have to show up in the right way. You have to have the mindset and the system. Your head has to be in the game and you have to follow the structure. And sometimes you're the only one who's going to get in the way.

I told you there was a time when I wasn't making any money. I told you that I needed to shift my focus and make a new decision. But what I didn't tell you were all of the things that were stopping me. First of all, I didn't have a topic and I didn't have a product. That was a problem for me and I was stuck. I didn't understand how my passion for personal development matched the marketplace. I was really passionate about helping people make change and if I connected one-on-one with someone, they got my passion, but I didn't know how to get that message out to the marketplace effectively. I just didn't know how to do that. Be honest with yourself if this is you, too.

I didn't have the right system. By the time I realized I should start presenting, I at least grasped the mindset of being an expert. But I didn't have these seven steps that I've shared with you because five years ago, no one was teaching this stuff. It was hard work for me to come up with it, but when I refined it, I knew it was good.

Before I had the system, feeling unprepared made me lack confidence. Sometimes I spoke on stage and people took action. Sometimes I spoke on stage and no one took action and I didn't know the difference. I was unprepared because I didn't have the same structure that I've shared with you. So then when I got up on stage, I'd get to the close and I'd start to get nervous thinking, "Is it going to work this time?" Do you know what I mean? I didn't have confidence through the close because I didn't know if it worked. My internal voice was on overdrive. "I should be getting this right. I've been studying personal development and speaking for so long. I should be making money." I beat myself up about it.

Another big one that stopped me was I was hearing so many speakers say, "I make a million dollars a year," and it seemed totally out of reach for me. I had no concept of that kind of money. This was back in the days when I was $19,000 in debt from investing in myself, doing all of those personal development trainings. I lived in scarcity. And to top it all off, I had major issues around sales. I didn't want to be a pushy salesperson so that held me back for a long time.

So over the years, all of those limiting beliefs really held me back. But my passion was strong enough to push me through my insecurities and my fears to get me where I am today. And my experience is not that different to everyone else's. Everyone has their different flavor. You'll have your own thing that's holding you back right now.

But remember Einstein? You can't solve the problem at the same level of thinking you were at when you created it. What's the missing link for you? What will take you from where you are to where you want to be right now? What shift do you need to make to get to the next level?

You have been introduced to a massive amount of information in this Blueprint, but if you set your mind to it, it's not going to take much to get started right away.

Let's look at what we covered:

1. We went through how to find and clearly articulate your passion.
2. We looked at how to find other people who share your passion, who are prospects for your business.
3. We looked at creating the core promise of your business.
4. We mapped out an Elegant Business Model for your business so every step you take fits into the overall plan.
5. We looked at how to propagate your message into the marketplace so you can start building your list today.
6. We looked at how to create an Effective Presentation that moves people to action in your business.
7. We talked about how to automate and leverage your business for maximum profit.

The Easy Way to Do It

If it all feels like it's too much to digest, don't be alarmed. I've crammed as much as I possibly could into this one book, but learning all of this material without someone to talk to about it can be pretty impractical.

That's why I'd like to invite you to join me on an upcoming webinar where we can go through this material in a relaxed way, and you can get some of your questions answered.

On the webinar we'll cover things like:

- The main reason most speakers fail
- How to apply the Seven Profit Principles in your industry
- How to decide which of the Profit Principles is the right place to start
- The fastest way to make new income within the next 30 days.

Starting a new direction like this can be daunting I know, but I'm totally committed to you achieving the very best you can for your business and your life. I hope I have the opportunity to help you integrate everything you've learned from the pages of this Blueprint. And the simplest way to start is by registering for the next webinar we have coming up.

You can do that here: www.presentationprofitsblueprint/nextstep.

If I do get to work with you, well then, see you soon and get ready to have some fun! If not, I truly hope that this book supports you in some small way to helping you to make the difference in the world that I know you were put on this planet to make.

See you on the platforms of the world.

ABOUT THE AUTHOR

Dr Joanna Martin is one of the world's most successful and inspirational speakers and educators, specializing in the field of entrepreneurialism and personal development. She has taught over 55,000 people on three continents (and counting!), captivating her audiences with an unusual combination of incredible intelligence, irreverent performer's attitude and genuine warmth.

Joanna's presentations and interviews are truly unique – as life changing as they are entertaining. Not only does she bring a quirky and feminine approach to an industry dominated by men, but she also provides proven systems, tools and models that empower people to create the life of their dreams. The results Joanna has helped her clients achieve to date are astonishing. Joanna's amazing story is an inspiration in itself. She started her working life as a medical doctor, after attaining first class honours at University. She then followed her heart into acting, training at the prestigious Actors Centre Australia (where Hugh Jackman and Nicole Kidman also trained). From there, Joanna's yearning to contribute as much as possible to the lives of others saw her launch a career as a speaker.

Joanna took her speaking business from a standstill to seven figures and two countries in just 12 months, and has made it her mission to teach others how to grow their business equally spectacularly while at the same time being true to their heart.

Now based between London and Melbourne with her husband Greg, Joanna is delighted to run what she calls "The Ultimate Lifestyle Business": Shift Speaker Training. Her corporate clients include ANZ Bank, Fairfax Publishing and eBay; and her speaking students include successful seven-figure speakers and numerous publicly recognised clients who prefer to keep their coaching confidential.

Spend more than a moment with Joanna and you will never forget her – and your life may never be the same!